What Did I Sign Up For?

Don't be a dick and other stories of a woman in a man's world, leading, learning, and driving change.

Kathleen Scudder

Dedication

This book is dedicated to all those fighting a constant uphill battle, beit big or small. Just keep swimming, never quit, and don't let anyone make you feel less than you are. Take care of yourself, most of all, because when you give too much of yourself, it takes a lot of effort to get it back.

Table of Contents

Introduction

I've been telling myself for years that I was going to write a book when I retire. Well, I retired, but I really don't know where to start. There are so many themes and ideas that come to my mind; should it be funny, serious? A leadership story, a woman's story, a cop's story, a poor-kid-who-did-ok kind of a story? My story encompasses all those things at once, and it turns out, I have a lot to say.

Some of this is going to be heavy and serious, but I'll throw some humor in there, and there is a lot of adventure and fun too. There will be cussing and sarcasm – so, hang on to your hooters (as my husband would say), we're going on the ride of my life.

My career path was not one of simply moving up traditionally, from one rung of the ladder to the next. It went like this:

1996-2004 (Nogales) - Supervisor for last 3 years.

2004-2007 (Erie) – Supervisor/National Recruiter for 2 years and a few months.

2007-2010 (Washington, DC) - Operations Officer for 1 year, and Assistant Chief for 2 years.

2010-2014 (Rio Grande Valley) – Field Operations Supervisor (FOS), Special Operations Supervisor (SOS), Assistant Chief Patrol Agent (ACPA), Deputy Patrol Agent in Charge (DPAIC) for one year each.

2014-2019 (San Diego) - ACPA, Division Chief - programs +COS, Patrol Agent in Charge (PAIC), Div Ch – Operations, Acting Deputy Chief Patrol Agent (DCPA).

2019-2020 (Washington, DC) – Associate Chief, Acting Dep Law Enforcement Operations Directorate (LEOD).

2020-2022 - CBP PARE – Executive Director.

2022-2024 - BP MSD – Executive Director.

Suffice it to say, I touched just about every rung on the career ladder of a Border Patrol Agent at some point. I learned a lot along the way and wouldn't go back and do much different.

Chapter 1
My Foundation

In early 1996, I was a senior in college, majoring in Criminal Justice. The only thing I wanted was to become a cop. Well, maybe not the only thing because I wanted a federal law enforcement job with good benefits and a good retirement. I wanted to be completely independent. Also, I really wanted to move out of New York State.

My father was in the Army until I was about maybe 7 or so, I can't remember exactly. Some memories are just not very clear, while others are incredibly vivid. I do remember moving from our lovely Victorian home near Watertown/Ft. Drum, New York to Vandalia, Illinois, where my father's family lived. It was 1982; I have no idea why I remember that year so clearly. My father was apparently out of work, had separated from the Army, and my mother had left her job because my father convinced her he had a job in Australia.

In addition, his story was so believable that our neighbors, my parents' best friends, were packing up and moving with us. We all got passports, went as far as to sell our house, and were ready to go when he decided to come clean.

I have one vivid memory in our van: my father was driving and crying--the slobbery uncontrollable kind of crying. I assumed it was shortly after he came clean. As the years progressed, things just got worse for their marriage.

After the Australia debacle, we had to go somewhere, so I moved to Vandalia, Illinois. Most of my father's family lived there—

he had like 10 brothers and sisters — and many still live there to this day.

The memories I have of our brief time there are of a severe concussion, where I vomited the entire drive to the hospital holding my head out the window of the car. I fell off my bike because there was a stick bug on my hand and those bugs freaked out my 8-year-old self. I remember feeling very alone and isolated because I was so shy that I only had one friend, who fell down our cellar stairs and never came over again. I received a beautiful, pink strawberry-flavored birthday cake and Barbie horse for my 8th birthday. It was the first year I had a cake of my own. My brother and I share a birthday, born one year apart — yes, we were the Irish twins.

My mother hated it there, and my father's air conditioning and heating business was fledgling. I realized things were bad when our car disappeared from in front of our house, re-possessed for non-payment. My mom wanted to go "home." New York State where she was born and raised.

We packed up again and moved back to New York. To an unknown, unfamiliar town near Rochester, named Clifton Springs, where I would spend the rest of my formative years until I left home for the Border Patrol Academy in 1996.

As we drove into town, the smell of rotten eggs hit every one of us in the car at the same time. "Ewwww, DAAAD," echoed from every one of us.

Running through the middle of downtown, Clifton Springs is a Sulfur Creek; the town, when founded, was known as Sulfur Springs. People used to believe that the sulfur in the water had healing properties and would flock to the town to wade in the springs. The solarium, where they would stay, stands today as apartments.

We moved in with a family that my parents had been connected to through our church. We stayed with this family until my parents found employment and got back on their feet. After several months, my parents found a rental home. It was uptown, which meant it was up the hill from downtown—where people lived in big, beautiful homes. There was only one street that went through town, from one end to the other—aptly named Main Street. Clifton Springs was a lovely historic town with a lot of charm. I appreciate that now.

My parents had to apply for food stamps (welfare) to support us. I remember my mother being incredibly ashamed that it had come to this.

She was a stubborn, proud woman who believed in hard work and didn't want to accept help, didn't want to *need* help.

They eventually found work with a small-town garage and local ambulance service, who sent them to training to become EMTs. My father was also a mechanic, so he worked in the garage in addition to becoming an EMT.

As months passed, I remember snippets of time:

Halloween, dressing as a Hobo in one of my father's flannel shirts and baggy jeans—this was probably the last year I went trick or treating.

My brother getting in trouble, ignoring me, and not wanting me around; annoying little sister.

The big front porch and my mom in the kitchen, angry or upset. Whatever it was, I didn't want to be around it, so I went somewhere, anywhere else. At least I had my room. I didn't like confrontation, I hated being yelled at, and mostly I didn't want to be in the way. I never heard my parents fight or argue. I can only remember the likely aftermaths of fights — my father would storm out and leave, and my mother would cry in her room, alone.

My brother dealt with a lot of this by acting out. He and I didn't get along for most of our childhood, as far as my memory serves. He was mean to me and I was a sensitive young child. I always felt like I had to try extra hard to make friends and I got picked on a lot, probably part of the reason for my intolerance of bullies to this day.

Eventually, my parents informed us that they bought a house, and we were moving. YAY — our own house. I knew this would make my mom feel better.

We were driving downtown though, the not-so-nice part of town. Maybe we would keep going, up the hill to the other side of town where the homes had a lot of land, or so we thought. Nope, we took a right onto Crane Street, smack dab in the center of town. Downtown was, more or less, a valley; the street lined with little shops, two hills on each side, both heading to the more residential streets with big houses and leading onward out of town. We passed the YMCA on our right and the Palace Theater on our left, a real working movie theater where I saw my first motion picture.

Two houses away, on the same side as the theater, we pulled up outside a house I knew of — a house I stayed away from because the dirtiest kid in school had lived there.

This was Billy Lockwood's house, and it was the ugliest, dirtiest, most run-down house in town.

The siding was made of green shingles, some of which were falling off. There were no closets, seemingly just open spaces between rooms. There was an upstairs, but no railing on the stairs or at the top that would prevent anyone from falling. Pretty much an attic. This eventually became my bedroom. I can remember hornets' nests in the ceiling, in the beams. I would just pray I never got stung when I went to sleep at night.

I couldn't be up there during the day in the summer—it was oppressively hot. My father promised us that he was going to fix it up, but he never fully came through. He put up paneling to cover the dirty walls. (oh yes, paneling), but not just plain old wood paneling, paneling with flowers on it, no doubt my mother's choice. He also started installing a wood stove in the kitchen, but that project never quite got finished.

This house would be the source of great embarrassment, depression, and bullying throughout my childhood, but a source of empathy, non-judgment, and understanding in my adulthood. Even today, I have dreams about fixing that house up for my mother.

Growing up in upstate New York was tough. The winters were brutal and the summers were stifling—very few people had air-conditioned homes. We certainly didn't. While my father was still around, both of my parents worked a lot just trying to make ends meet. As EMTs at a small-town ambulance service, they were subject to call-outs at all hours of the day and night. I don't remember my mother or my father having hobbies or outside interests. They worked, did what they could for their kids, and attempted to find moments of rest throughout.

I remember Christmas morning one year—sometime in the 80s—my brother and I, not-so-patiently were waiting to open presents until my parents returned from a call. We both took peeks around the tree to see what we could see.

We had already been allowed to come downstairs, so the surprise was over, but we had not settled in to open the presents yet when the phone rang, and my parents had to go. I think that was "the year of the Cabbage Patch." I have a very vivid memory of one sitting right out in front of the tree, unwrapped — because gifts from Santa were not wrapped in my house, that was the tradition.

Things were pretty good then, from my child's eye perspective. I mean, the tree was surrounded by gifts and my father was still around. For years to come, and until her death, my mom always made Christmas special.

In 1986, the first of many health tragedies befell my mother. I was 12 years old when my mother had a major heart attack and nearly died. She was barely 42 and just had her birthday.

It was a Saturday in May, and she had taken my brother and me to breakfast at the local diner. She was well-known around town as she was one of the only few EMTs — dressed in her whites as they wore back then and her fluorescent orange jacket — the colors of the ambulance service. Even the ambulances had a bright orange stripe along the side.

My father, as far as I knew, was working somewhere away, having supposedly gotten back into the Army as a reservist. After we got home from breakfast, my mom said she felt nauseous and went into the bathroom. Shortly thereafter, she was on the floor breathlessly calling to my brother or me to call the ambulance, she was having a heart attack. One of us called, I don't remember which, but they were taking forever so I ran down the street to the ambulance service to get them to hurry up.

I mean, this woman works with you, what is taking so long? We lived only 3 houses away.

One of the EMTs followed me on foot back to our house. The ambulance finally arrived, and they took her away. As I was following the gurney out of the house with my mother on it, I remember seeing Mrs. Lincoln, the mom of one of my friends from girl scouts, getting out of her car and heading up to our house. She took me with her back to her house. She somehow heard what was going on and came as quickly as she could.

The good thing about small towns is everyone knows each other, and they tend to take care of each other. The bad thing about small towns is everyone knows each other, and everyone knows your business.

My mom was in the ICU for what seemed like a very long time. My brother and I ended up staying with separate family friends — so we were not together anymore. Even after my father came home, I stayed at the Lincolns' house with my friend, Heather. At some point, a few days later, I remember being taken to the hospital to visit my mom. They brought my brother and me into the ICU, not a place where children were typically allowed.

The first thing I saw when I walked into the room was the ventilator, the accordion-looking thing, inside a clear tube moving up and down. When I think of that day, that is the vision I see. My mom was on the bed with all the hoses hooked up to her and immediately to the right was the ventilator, breathing for her. The nurses explained what it was doing so we wouldn't be scared. We were still scared.

I know now that this visit was to say goodbye because they did not expect my mom to make it.

She had other ideas, the tenacious woman that she was. She pulled through. My father came home very briefly during that time and maybe stayed around another year, on and off. He would be home for a period and go away for a period, but eventually, I became the caretaker of my mother. And he never came home again.

The last time I remember seeing my father was when I was 14 and involved in a pretty serious car accident with another close friend, Tammy, and her sister. My mother must have gotten a hold of him and convinced him to come home. His baby girl—as I was told later, I was the apple of his eye—was hurt.

He showed up for what seemed like a few minutes, and I have not seen him since. So much for being the apple of his eye.

Things got pretty desperate from then on. This accident led to one physical ailment that impacted the rest of my life—my spine. I'm pretty sure the hospital staff should have at least taken X-rays because I had to be carried out of the emergency room before being released. I recall, when I stood up to walk, I had excruciating pain in my lower back, down my left leg—but they never did notice, or cared enough to notice. That sciatic pain plagues me to this day. I eventually had three different surgeries on my lower back—the last of which was a spinal fusion when I was in my late 40s. I never let any of that slow me down though.

This isn't meant to be my life's sad story, but I give this detail to set the foundation. I grew up with some challenges and the older I got, the worse the home situation became. My brother and I did not get along and we would fight, physically fight, on occasions. It always ended up with me crying and him begging me to not tell Mom.

We were dirt poor. The local church leaving boxes of food and clothing on your front porch kind of poor. The electric company turning off the electricity in upstate New York in January kind of poor, and again in February and again in March. The kind of poor where my mother did not know how she was going to provide for her two teenagers, so she took a job babysitting the kids across the street for $40 a week, post-heart attack and leg amputation (that's a whole other story).

The roof leaked, the basement flooded and there was nothing we could do but kick the sump pump after wading through knee-high water and put pots all around the house. The cellar floor was dirt and I was certain there was a monster in the dark corner of the basement because there was no light except over the decrepit staircase, so you always had to bring a flashlight, which never fully lit. The drop ceiling went throughout the house—a cheap way to cover up any problems on the real ceiling, and it did just that. Once rain leaked into those panels and they became so saturated, they dropped with a splash of dirty rainwater all over the living room carpet. *I dread rain to this day.*

And the bugs...*shiver…*

It was the worst house on the block, maybe in the town. In fact, that house was razed after my mom finally could not hold on to it financially and moved to Arizona to live with me. That turned out to be a blessing in disguise for many reasons.

The circumstances of my youth led me to focus on two goals, initially—I wanted to be able to afford a car that ran and make enough money to heat my home in the winter. I vowed to myself that I would do well enough to not want those two things, and break the cycle of women in my family being financially dependent on a man. This childhood forged me into the person I am today.

In hindsight, it was an incredible foundation because even through all the struggles, there were many lessons and lots of love. I didn't come from money or luck; I came from hard work. No one gave me anything. I made choices that led to success, I took opportunities when they presented themselves and I didn't make excuses. I stayed out of trouble; oh, I made mistakes, but I earned everything, the good and the bad.

So anyway, back to 1996. I was a senior in college and focused on a job in law enforcement. I had taken multiple tests for the local Sheriff's department, New York State Corrections, Rochester City Police — you name it, I was applying for it. My friend, Heather, and I for sure thought we would be Cagney and Lacey someday. I was the only one to follow the law enforcement path though.

Back in the mid-90s, you had to pretty much score 100 on those tests to even be considered. There were 100s of people testing for the Rochester Police back then. I can remember testing in a cafeteria at some large school and it was FULL. I do not remember my exact score on any of the tests, but it was not 100, I do remember that. I had grand illusions of going into the DEA or the FBI because what college kid majoring in Criminal Justice doesn't? Turned out, they require a little more than a bachelor's degree in criminal justice.

In fact, a DEA recruiter at a Criminal Justice focused job fair informed me that a Criminal Justice degree was a worthless degree. The FBI recruiter stated that the FBI was looking for people with accounting degrees at that time, and you needed three years of full-time work experience before applying to the FBI.

Awesome, too late to change my major. I was graduating in a month, and I needed a job.

At the same job fair, over in the corner, stood two recruiters in green uniforms (my favorite color at the time). I had never seen that uniform before — bright gold lettering spelling out 'The U.S. Border Patrol' on a deep blue background, overlaying a golden outline of the United States of America. Simple, but something I came to adore and feel protective of. I had never heard of the Border Patrol. I approached them and began speaking with the recruiter and **she** (remember this, I'll come back to it later) said two things that absolutely resonated with me — **Arizona** and **Federal**.

I asked, "Where do I sign up?"

I was all about leaving NY to anywhere warmer. They were hiring in Arizona, California, and Texas — yes, please. I took home the paperwork and filled it out in black pen, as required. It was a million-page application. Ok, maybe not a million pages, but it was long. I mailed it in and waited.

A few weeks later, I heard back, via US Mail, and this was what I saw in the letter — Philadelphia, Pennsylvania. This is where I had to go to take the test.

I didn't have a car. I didn't even have a valid driver's license.

My mom forgot to mail in the plates to her car, which was registered in my name, and NY State punishes you by suspending your license for this infraction. Never mind that I also had points on my license from a few speeding tickets. Oopsy. It was suspended for 6 months. The car we had probably wouldn't have made the trip anyway.

My mom and I took the Amtrak train for 8 hours from Rochester, NY to Philadelphia, PA.

This was during a time when the agency was doing what they termed expedited hiring, wherein everything was done in one weekend. They proctored the test on Saturday morning; if you passed, you would move on to the interview the following day. If you passed that, you immediately had your fingerprints taken to begin the background investigation and then straight to the doctor, uptown somewhere in Philly, for your physical.

Chapter 2
The Test

The test was a multiple-choice reasoning and general grammar, can you think in a straight line, kind of civil service exam. However, to become a Border Patrol Agent, you must also learn to speak, write, and UNDERSTAND the Spanish language.

Yeah, so, I took 4 years of German in high school and no foreign language in college. To this day, I cannot recite the Spanish alphabet in its entirety and always end up finishing in German. To evaluate whether or not a non-native speaker can learn Spanish, they have what is called an artificial language test. Native Spanish speakers take a Spanish test instead. The Artificial language test involves essentially non-sense words, and one must follow the rules to interpret the language. Yes, it is very strange. They did provide some practice materials ahead of time, which did not make it any less confusing.

Somehow, I ended up passing the test and if my memory serves me, I scored somewhere in the 80s. Good enough to progress to the next step.

The Interview

The interview would be performed the following day at your given time in the same hotel. They expected you to arrive on time, in appropriate attire — uh oh, what does that mean? It was the 90s and flannel was the shiznit. I did not bring, much less own, a single "professional" piece of clothing. I had my "nice flannel" but I already wore that for the test.

Have I mentioned that I was shy, withdrawn, introverted and my self-confidence was approximately zero?

I was required to participate in an internship during college, so I chose to do one with the Rochester Police Department. Part of that internship involved participating with the community in a group called Police and Citizens Together Against Crime (PACTAC). We would put on our little blue and yellow safety vests with the letters PACTAC on them and walk around the community keeping an eye on things and calling in anything suspicious. The police officer running the program told me, "You will never make it as a cop if you don't find a way to come out of your shell." Um, ok, duly noted. I came out of my friggin' shell alright.

Back in Philly, I had to get a cab, in a city I had never been to, with my mom, who was in a wheelchair, and to get clear across town to the mall. The front desk recommended it to find and buy a suit for the interview the next morning.

My mom, probably using her last dime, paid for the cab and bought me a very nice, expensive suit and matching shoes. Yippy, I'm a big girl now. The suit was a navy blue skirt with a white jacket that had navy blue on the lapel and pockets. I can still see it in my head. I wore this suit to every single "professional" event for several years to come.

A quick note here on my mom. Her story is in and of itself a tragedy and a triumph. Perhaps one day, I will write it. Suffice it to say, she was my biggest cheerleader, my biggest supporter, she did her best and she taught me, through her actions, to have **ZERO** *quit in my grit. 'Can't' was not a term she displayed or embodied. She was an amazing woman who dealt with, and overcame, incredible obstacles.*

It was a Sunday morning, and I was preparing for the interview. I was a heavy Mountain Dew drinker at that time, so I prepared by downing at least two before I headed downstairs to the assigned room. 'That will surely calm my nerves.'

I had absolutely no idea what to expect. I was told it was a panel interview, but I really didn't know what that even meant.

I walked into the room and there were 3 older men (I was 22, everyone was older), in full dress uniform (Class A for those who understand that speak) seated behind a table with binders of what seemed like reams of paper in front of them. They wore shiny black leather belts and shiny gold badges.

I was intimidated.

My memory tells me they were all balding and portly, but I'm not 100% sure if that's accurate. Perhaps that was just how I put them in their place today, having lived through 27 years with the agency. I do remember they all had mustaches. I don't know what it is about the Border Patrol and mustaches, but everyone seemed to have them in the 90s, and now again in the 2020s.

I noticed nothing else in the room but a single chair situated a few feet from the table. I took my seat. I was in the spotlight, and I was all alone. This feeling will become a theme throughout my career, if not just a feeling rather than a true situation. I have never enjoyed being the center of attention.

They asked some biographical questions, if I had any relatives in the patrol, and then we began. They provided three scenarios, one at a time, to which they provided several follow-up questions. I remember two of the scenarios, though not very clearly, and nothing of the third.

The first scenario had something to do with being on an airplane, responding to traffic somewhere over the desert. However, the plane crashed and, as the situation would have it, the plane was on fire. I was the only one conscious and the radios were not working.

'Really? Ok. Let me have it, let's do this.'

I provided an answer that involved putting someone in a tourniquet and trying to pull them to safety across the desert, by myself, on a makeshift gurney (I must be Wonder Woman). Well, turned out I had really screwed that one up.

"So, you're a hero," one of the men said.

I was like, Errr, no. God, can I please just be anywhere else right now? I did my very best to hold back tears of embarrassment and I could tell that they were keyed in on this. They were staring at me, burrowing their eyes into my soul, waiting for me to provide an alternate answer, or start crying. I had nothing.

I remember one of them suggesting something and I grasped onto it. He had graciously thrown me a bone — 'Yes, sir, that is exactly what I would do. I'm going to wait near the wreckage because it's on fire and surely someone will see the smoke billowing into the air and send help.'

Yikes, what could possibly be next?

The next scenario was situated at a bus station. They set it up:

"You are in a bus station, there are tens of people around, flittering about and you are faced with an individual who has you backed against the wall because he does not appreciate your line of questioning. You can't reach your radio to call for backup."

(Again, really?) It seemed like every scenario I ever heard about involved radios not working.

"What do you do? The subject is becoming increasingly aggressive and physical. What are you going to do, WHAT ARE YOU GOING TO DO?"

Well, I don't want to be a hero again, that was clearly frowned upon. I thought I knew exactly what I would do, but I was also trying to figure out how to say it professionally. And then I said to myself, 'Just say it.'

"I will knee them in the balls, as hard as I can."

Complete and utter silence.

Bingo, BOOM. Take that.

They all looked a little uncomfortable, sheepish even, as they adjusted their seated positions — just a tad. That was the end of the interview. No further questions. They began feverishly writing notes on their stacks of paper and I was excused. I headed just outside this room to wait for the verdict.

An eternity later, one of the men exited the room, handed a paper to another person awaiting the results, and, invited me back into the room. I don't remember much of what they said other than I passed.

Before I was excused for the second time, one of the men with a somewhat crooked smile on his face mentioned that they recognized I held it together when things got heated and uncomfortable.

Oh, I did? If you say so. I was dying inside. 'WHEW! I passed! Oh My God, I Passed!' Internal happy dance.

The Physical Exam

The physical exam was being given that afternoon, again, across town. Well, Christ, now, I had to find a cab again. I was told they would want a urine sample, but I didn't have to pee because the stress of the last hour or so had dehydrated me.

I downed a few more cans of my favorite beverage, Mt. Dew, hailed a cab—for the second time in my life, without my mom this time—and I was on my way. They did all the physical stuff: took my blood pressure, asked all the past health-related questions, and performed an EKG.

Remember those four Mt. Dews I had that morning? Apparently, caffeine combined with a shit ton of stress hormones can make your heart do funky things. Who knew? I would have to re-take the EKG at some point.

I had to hail a cab again, this time to get back to the hotel. So, in my nice lady suit, I stepped out into traffic, my hand in the air, and hailed a cab, just like I'd seen on TV. I was a big city girl. I re-took the EKG sans Mt. Dew at my personal doctor later but everything turned out fine.

The Background Investigation.

Remember the billion-page application? (Maybe it was only a million.) That was also information for the background investigation.

I was a good kid, and drank a bit, but I *was* in college, and I played Rugby, so, that should be understandable. From a young age, probably at least in middle school, I knew that I wanted to be in law enforcement. So, I never once tried any kind of illegal drug, not marijuana, not even cigarettes; even when my friends did, I abstained. I was admittedly a square. I stayed out of any kind of trouble. I expected this to go quickly and without issue, which it did.

Each time my investigator visited a friend or family member, they called to let me know. They thought this was pretty cool. The only thing that concerned me was that my brother got in some trouble here and there, and I didn't know how that may impact the background. Turned out to be just fine. He didn't continue that path forever; he's a good man now!

The Job Offer

The whole process, in hindsight, went at lightning speed, considering we are talking about the Federal government. It only took five months from the time I spoke to the recruiter to my first day on duty.

However, I was starting to stress as I had not heard anything, even though I knew the investigator had spoken to all my friends and family. Around the first part of September, having just found my third part-time job and seeking anything full-time that I possibly could, I worked up the courage to call the number the agency provided to inquire about the status of my application.

Remember that whole license plate/suspended license thing? That was what was holding up the offer.

The lady on the other end of the phone asked if my license suspension was over, to which I could thankfully reply yes—I literally got it back that week. Two weeks later, I received the letter in the mail that I had eagerly been awaiting. They were assigning me to Arizona—woohoo, my first choice—in a border town called Nogales. Say it with me: NO GALEs. Long O, long A, two syllables, because that is how you pronounce it in English if you do not know the pronunciation rules of the Spanish language.

Giddy with excitement—as much as any introvert could be (internal jump)—I called my mom, of course, and then immediately called my best friend, Heather. I told her I was going to NO GALES, Arizona.

"Didn't you and Steve (her husband) just go to Arizona?" I asked. She paused and said, very sarcastically, because that is how we hug where I come from, "Do you mean No *gal* es? Long O, short A, short E, pronounce all 3 syllables and every letter."

"Um…sure, that place." My very first Spanish lesson.

I was to report in two weeks. I had to quit three jobs, and oh yeah, I still didn't have a car of my own. My mother was driving me to and from work as we were sharing a car. The academy was in Charleston, South Carolina, but first I had to get to Tucson, Arizona, on my own dime, to enter on duty where I would be stationed. And then, Government would then fly the whole class to the academy.

I had never been west of the Mississippi, and I had only flown once, in high school, on a band trip to Florida. How do you even buy a plane ticket?

I got my first credit card that summer. My mom thought it would be a good idea if I started building credit—thankfully, because I had no idea how to pay for a plane ticket with cash. There was no internet yet. I figured it out.

Our good family friend, Robin, went with us to the airport, and I remember telling them, "I don't think I want to go". They both reassured me that I would be fine. I wasn't sure what the heck I was getting myself into, but I knew that I could not fail — not because it wasn't possible, but because there was too much riding on me making it through the academy. I cried when I left my mom.

I just want to carve a minute out here to talk about Robin, Gary, her husband, and their daughter, Jessica — because I wouldn't be where or who I am without the crucial role they played in my life.

When I was 15, the only job I could really do was babysitting. I had a few regular "clients," if you will, and many of my friends also babysat. My friend, Heather, and her family were very well-known throughout the town.

One day, a young woman called me, indicating that she had gotten my name from Sue Lincoln, Heather's mom, as someone who may be available and interested in a full-time babysitting job. Four days a week for $60. Hell, yes, this is what I was hoping for. The young woman was Robin. Robin came to my house (the horrible green one on Crane Street) to pick me up for my "interview" and to meet her husband and her daughter.

Robin was a pretty, blonde woman, young to the appearance, 28 at the time if my memory serves me. Their house was only a few streets away, maybe a 10-minute walk. We pulled up outside their house – white with green shutters on the front bay window – I thought it was the cutest house. She showed me inside and there was a little girl, Jessica, with an older man, who I automatically assumed was her grandfather – until Robin introduced me to her husband, Gary. Oopsy. Thou shalt not judge thy book by its cover, Kathleen. Robin and Gary had a pretty decent age difference, and it turned out that didn't matter a damn bit.

I was hired and on my first day, I was promptly handed several pages of handwritten rules. Pages, plural. Front and back. They really had some issues with the last babysitter. My first thought was 'oh my god, lady, calm down.' Not a problem, I was a rule follower and I stayed out of trouble.

Over time, this family and my family became very close. Robin taught me how to drive and she provided counsel and mentorship as I became a young woman. My mom became Jessica's adopted grandmother. After I went away to college, my mother took over the care of Jessica. Gary taught me how to shoot just before I left for the Academy. He took my brother hunting. Gary walked me down the aisle when I got married. Robin and Jessica were also in my wedding. Robin and Gary are my daughter's godparents. We spent holidays together. They welcomed my husband into the fold without hesitation. Family really is so much more than blood.

Gary was a cop and I think that really impressed upon me some particular values. I saw how they lived their lives, and I emulated a lot of it. Gary passed away in 2007 from cancer. It was a tough blow, another close loss. Robin, Jess, and my family are still close and stay in touch very often and we will forever consider each other family. They say people come in and out of your life, some stay for a season, but these people are forever. I have a few of those, and I consider myself very lucky.

Chapter 3
The Academy

On September 25, 1996, I arrived at the Tucson Sector office on Ajo Way in Tucson, Arizona to enter on duty (EOD) as a Border Patrol Agent with the 322nd session of the United States Border Patrol Academy.

By this time, I was obviously a pro at getting a cab, so the morning we had to report, I reserved a cab and told the driver, I needed to go to Ajo Way. Say it with me — A (short A), JOE (long O) Way.

My second Spanish lesson involved the driver explaining to this Gringa (white girl) that a J in Spanish is pronounced like an H. He chuckled, looked at me in the rearview mirror and very politely (or so I assume) said, "Do you mean A (short A) Ho?" Yes, of course, that was what I meant. Thank you, kind sir, I'll never forget it.

The next few days involved a ton of paperwork and a trip to the station where we would be assigned. There were approximately 25 individuals who EOD'd in Tucson, 5 of whom were going to be assigned with me in Nogales. The six of us got in a van with a few Border Patrol Agents from Nogales and proceeded down Interstate 19 for the 70-ish miles from Tucson to Nogales.

The scenery was dry and desert-like. I saw my first saguaro cactus; you know the one, shown in all the western cartoons and movies. The ones that look like they have their arms raised doing the robot dance. Turns out, Tucson is one of, if not the only, place they grow. I had never seen the desert before and I thought it was beautiful. It was also September and in the 80s — absolute heaven.

That Wednesday, we boarded a plane to Charleston, South Carolina to attend the academy at the Federal Law Enforcement Training Center's (FLETC) satellite facility; 19 fun-filled weeks of Naturalization and Immigration law, defense tactics, pursuit driving, shooting, Physical Training (PT), running, Statutory, Constitutional and Criminal law, more running, push-ups...and I almost forgot, boxing and more push-ups.

We landed in Charleston, and I noticed that my group was only half the class. The remaining 25 or so would be assigned to the El Paso Sector.

There was a bus waiting to take us to the Academy. It was late afternoon, more like early evening and it had been a pretty long day already. When we arrived at the academy, I looked out the window and saw a line of very fit men in their dress uniforms, wearing Smokey the Bear hats pulled down as far on their foreheads as possible. They looked very intimidating; military-like – one in particular – a very muscular black man with a menacing face and loud booming voice. He turned out to be one of our law instructors and, actually, a very kind man. Once my classmates began deboarding the bus, I could hear them being yelled at and all I could think was, **"What the hell did I sign up for**? Was this the military after all? I did not sign up for the Army."

Someone may have mentioned this was a paramilitary organization but what I had paid attention to so far was that I was going to get a paycheck and health benefits and I'd be moving to Arizona. And what does paramilitary even mean? I obviously didn't know.

They were yelling at us to get in line, straighten up, "Now go get your bags, and get up to your rooms. Hurry up, move it, trainee." I guess we had the room assignment information somewhere; I have no recollection of how I knew where to go. All I can remember is scrambling to carry the three burdensome pieces of luggage that contained every piece of clothing I owned. The straps were broken on one, and the suitcase I had did not roll; a wheel got broken sometime during the trip. So, I was just tripping over myself and carrying three very awkward-looking bags, trying to run and not get yelled at or noticed.

I was the only female amongst the agents-to-be that were in the Tucson group. This would become yet another theme throughout my career – the only female in the room. There were two other females in my class, but they were going to be assigned to the El Paso Sector, so I had not met them yet.

I finally made it to my room. My roommate – a red-headed, slender woman, stood up from her bed, said, "Hi, I'm Mary" and proceeded to hand me a beer. 'God Bless her,' I thought, 'we shall get along just fine.'

On the first day of classes, we all walked into a classroom and saw nothing but stacks of books and binders on our desks. Immigration law has volumes upon volumes. We were given a Spanish placement test to determine which group we would be assigned to. I knew two Spanish words, Nogales and Ajo. They weren't on the test, so the only writing on my page was my name and that's German and Irish.

There would be six groups. Group one was the native Spanish speakers. I was placed in group 6 – the equivalent of kindergarten class-level learning. Thankfully, I had an aptitude to learn the language and I spent most of my homework time either memorizing

Spanish vocabulary with my other group 6 classmates, or quizzing my roommate as she quizzed me on Immigration Law. After the mid-term exam, they shifted some folks around and I graduated to group 5. I ended up scoring in the upper 90s on all the exams. Could I speak and understand the language? As long as people were using the words I had learned, I did ok. I lost those skills over the years as I used them less and less. Classic case of "If you don't use it, you lose it." I can get by well enough to not get myself into trouble today, but that is pretty much it.

The academy curriculum has since changed, particularly in PT, but in the '90s, we ended our PT doing the one thing it seemed we were preparing for the entire time – hand-to-hand combat, in the form of boxing. I remember throwing up that morning,

Our opponents were decided by weight, and I have never been light. I describe myself as dense – I didn't look as heavy as I was. Add the muscle I'd gained over the last 19 weeks, and I would be boxing a triathlete. A dude. A man. Mike.

All of the females had to box males, as a matter of fact. I do remember though, that the guys we boxed then had to box a male of equal weight. Of course, there were those guys who thought it would be awesome to see us females fight it out, c'mon dude, this isn't mud wrestling. Boys will be boys. I realize that someone may be thinking, that's not ok. No, it wasn't ok, and I know that now. I knew it then, but we all rolled our eyes, and we just went with the flow. None of us wished to be singled out for any reason.

I was always nervous before PT, but this was the worst I had felt...ever. The PT instructors were the militant, fit guys we encountered getting off the bus the first day. They were tough on us, they yelled and picked on you if you stood out – very intimidating behavior. The mindset was to break you down as a team and build you back up as a team. If one person screwed up, everyone paid for it.

We all stood out because we were three females among 47 men. Mary and I stood out because we were two red-headed, single white girls from the northeast. Mary came from Philly and I was from New York. The Border Patrol was made up of over 50% Hispanic males, at this time and 97% male overall. White females were unicorns.

Of us two redheads and a smallish Hispanic female, she was the one they picked on the most. I guess she was an easy target. She was injured early on and thus struggled in PT. She got into the BP after originally being denied because they found out she was pregnant, as did she, at her physical exam. She filed against the government until finally the US Attorney at the time, Janet Reno, decided on her case, and she entered the patrol.

We were entering into an organization that was heavy in Hispanic machismo culture, combined with type A personalities while also being on the southwest border. To the men, we were a prize, and to other women, we were a competition. This was a whole new experience for me.

I was quiet, and shy, did not consider myself attractive by any stretch, and my self-confidence was still zero. The powers that be, at least, saw fit to put all of us females in the same group, as they split the class in two, Group A and B, so we had each other to lean on. I came straight out of college into the patrol as if starting another semester of college, except I was earning a paycheck this time. They were paying me, not the other way around.

Back to boxing — my partner did not want to box a female.

Mike was a genuinely nice guy, married already with kids. He was one of the more mature guys in the class and had some life experience. This was not his thing, and he was not going to enjoy it a single bit. He was top of the class in PT, and did I mention he was a competing triathlete?

Before the start of the match, while putting on my gear, one of the instructors who I will NEVER forget approached me. His nickname was El Diablo (the devil), and he earned every syllable of that nickname. The other two females had already boxed, and both came out of the ring in tears. He got right up in my scared 22-year-old face and said, as harshly, but hushed as he could, "RICKMAN YOU BETTER NOT CRY." Well, shit, I wanted to cry right now, you asshole. Alright, let's do this.

We put on our gear and stepped into the makeshift ring. We danced around a bit, took some shots at each other and then I heard from the corner, "You better hit her, and you better mean it." I had never been hit in the face or the head and the nausea that morning was proof that I knew I would be, and I did not know how I would react.

Mike didn't really have a choice, so he obliged and hit me square in the head and I went down, immediately.

He rushed over to me and said "I'm so sorry, I'm so sorry." The instructors interceded, and checked me out. I got right back up, but it stunned me for sure. We concluded our match and Mike embraced me with the tightest, almost choke-like hold, as we walked out of the mat room. He kept my head down and I think it was to shelter me from onlookers. I was doing my damndest to hold back tears because I would NOT let them see me cry. I did not cry. And if even a tear flowed down my cheek, no one would have seen it because Mike wouldn't let me go until we got out of the room.

I would run into El Diablo later in my career, after being in the field for a few years. I was tasked to pick up a group of detailers (agents coming into town to work our area from other areas of the country) from the airport and while waiting in the baggage claim area — who walked off the plane?

He recognized me and I him. He proceeded, in his machismo, cocky way to tell me to get his bags. I laughed out loud and told him, "I'm not a trainee anymore, you can get your own bags." He immediately changed his attitude, as bullies do when challenged. I'd dealt with bullies my whole life and I was done with that.

I had found my confidence and self-worth, mostly. I would make one feel small and completely emasculate a bully. I started doing it in High School. Wrong, right, or indifferent, you set the parameters of how you allow people to treat you and those around you. I will forever root for the underdog and stand up against bullies.

Mary and I, to this day, meet up every year or so to go on a girls' trip. Moms only, no kiddos, and we always have a great time catching up and making new memories together.

I've kept track of most of my classmates and know where many of them are even today — most retired or left the patrol. The academy, I came to realize, was the one team-building exercise that every Border Patrol Agent went through. It was our common place. The thing that began to connect and bind us to one another from day one. This was where we all proved that we belonged and every one of us went through the same experience.

Agents come from all walks of life and backgrounds, but every single Border Patrol Agent has the academy in common.

The Academy was tough, physically and academically, but ultimately a very positive experience. I was woefully out of shape, and not a runner up to that point, so PT was very hard. I was close to the back of the pack on every run. Immigration Law gave me a run for my money as well, so I knew I had to buckle down and focus. I have mostly good memories and it was the first time in my career, maybe my life, that I accomplished something I really did not know that I could.

What is this feeling…confidence? I was on my way.

Chapter 4
Male Domination

In the mid-90s, women had only been allowed to be in the field in most of law enforcement for about 20 years. It was sometime in the 70s when the first women graduated from the Border Patrol Academy—considered one of the toughest law enforcement academies. The requirements for successful completion of the academy for men and women are exactly the same. When I joined the USBP, there were around 3% women. In the 1970s, women accounted for roughly 2 percent of sworn officers, primarily holding clerical positions, nationwide. Today, they make up only 13 percent of the force, nationwide, particularly in larger departments. (Public/Private Sector Partnerships for Community Preparedness (usdoj.gov)

The USBP arguably had, and still has, the lowest ratio of females to males. The USBP has increased their percentage of women, in the last 27 years (the tenure of my career) to just above 6% as of 2023. I don't know if that growth percentage is considered good or not, but at least it has increased. Law enforcement in general is a male-dominated field and, frankly, not as many women are attracted to this line of work. Or it is not cut out for them, their needs, preferences, or priorities. Add to that already difficult list of requirements the restrictions you face when entering the USBP.

First, you must start your career on the southwestern border. This has changed, very recently, but the majority of the work is still on the Southern border. That means you must move, paid for by you, sometimes thousands of miles to an unknown place, culture, and environment with no family, friends, or support system. I packed my cookies and my Scottish Terrier, McDuff, in my brand-new Chevy Blazer and trucked across the nation for this job.

Being the only female in the room was incredibly common. It can be intimidating, but over time, I rarely noticed it anymore. I didn't pay much attention to that fact at all for a long time unless someone pointed it out. I just wanted to do my job, get along with my co-workers, and frankly, learn all I could while having a good time and protecting America.

From my perspective, I was just an agent, like all the men.

I didn't want to be singled out for being female, given anything, or have anything additional or special expected of me. I did want to be respected and that the expectations of me were because I was a good agent. Being considered "one of the guys" was a compliment. I was naïve and oblivious. It worked for me. I developed friendships and work relationships, and a good reputation as a hard worker. It was ok for the guys to joke around with me, I gave as good as I got. I did not see it as harassing or menacing. They certainly pushed the limits sometimes to see how far they could go, but I was never one to hold back in telling them to knock it off. My first work unit was pretty awesome, and I still keep in contact with many people from those early years.

The only other female in my first work unit was a supervisor. She was hard. In fact, all the senior females at the station were hard or hardened by life, the job, and the environment. There were probably fewer than 10 females at the station when I arrived. Most of us had arrived in the last 2-3 years. The Border Patrol had a huge hiring push in the mid-nineties.

The women were hard on each other and probably hard on themselves. If you couldn't cut it and were in any way giving females a bad name or reputation, you were absolutely ostracized for it. You better keep your head down and do your damn job. There was no real sisterhood amongst the women, certainly not like I see now. I remember the next female that came onto my unit was one hundred-star numbers behind me. I was November (phonetic for N – Nogales) 385 and she was N 485. For the longest time, we were the only two in our unit and we were ironically both named Kathy.

She and I became friendly, and the supervisors often paired us to work together. She and I found common ground in our love for furry creatures. We rescued dogs in between answering calls, not intentionally, but stray dogs were everywhere. More on that topic in another chapter.

As time went on, I began to recognize that as a woman who was advancing in my career, whether I wanted to or not, I was an example for other females and other agents, period.

For a long time, I was one of those females who thought I was just another agent. I didn't want to admit that I was treated differently or acknowledge that we needed something different. Very much on accident, I realized that it came down to equity. Equality provides the same opportunities for everyone. Equity takes into consideration a person's environment, culture, personal life, and what they are up against or dealing with when provided those opportunities. For example, a single parent has far more challenges than most two-parent households. Simply providing a single parent with the opportunity (equality) to advance or move, doesn't cover all the bases. They must figure out how to make that opportunity fit into their lives or fit their lives into that opportunity and there is no consideration for the challenges that will create. Such as midnight shifts as a single parent on the border, with no support system.

The attitude of the agency is you figure it out, we pay you to do a job and you signed up for shift work. What I am trying to say is that men and women may be equal—in theory. But we are not the same. We are biologically different. We have different inherent strengths, attitudes, and approaches to life. Like it or not, society still has different expectations of men and women. I'm not saying that is good or bad, it just is.

To prove my point, here is a list of things men will never have said to them, but that I—and probably most other females of my generation—have heard more than once (and my responses for a giggle):

- You should smile more; you look pretty when you smile. (Please go fuck yourself.)
- Do they let you wear a gun? (Yes, and I go out after dark without a chaperone too.)
- Do they let you go out in the field? (OMG, that is what the gun is for.)
- Are you going to stay home after you have the baby? (No, but I'm going to bring the baby with me so I can breastfeed her on shift.)
- You only got the job/position/promotion because they had to hire a female. (Thanks, then why did they ever promote you?)
- Who is taking care of your kids if you're working? (No one, I put them in cages when I leave the house.)
- Who is the boss at home? (C'mon dude—who is the boss at your home?)
- How do you do it all? (I don't and there is always a sacrifice.)

Seriously—please find me 2 men who were ever asked any of those questions.

Chapter 5
Creepers and Peepers

The Border Patrol, as it turns out, is—and this is a strictly made up, personal opinion statistic—85% good hard-working people, 10% lazy slugs, some downright ugly individuals who are just angry at the world, and a very small percentage of straight up criminals— legitimate murderers, rapists, child porn sickos, predators, voyeurs, and child abusers. That small percentage really puts a nasty stain on the agency. Those in the middle, I called them *creepy*. Women will understand, better than anyone, the very specific meaning of the word creepy. These are the people you try to avoid. They look through you, not at you and they rarely make eye contact.

I firmly believe you never really know someone unless you have worked for them or lived with them. My experiences throughout my 27-year career support this theory repeatedly. Beyond that, people tend to purport themselves to be who they want you to think they are.

Someone once described the Border Patrol culture as a little "rapey." I have to say that by and large, that was not my experience. As I look back there were certainly circumstances that would not be tolerated by today's standards. I chalked it up to boys being boys. I handled it. I guessed they were just treating me like one of the guys, I was like their little sister, right? If they were picking on me, it meant they liked me, right? More than once, someone would give me that look and ask, "Can I tell you something—I want to say something, but I don't want it to be weird?" Nope, please don't, because then it would be weird. Time to go, I think they just called me on the radio.

No one ever tried to rape me. Let me be very clear on that point. I know, however, that there were women who experienced some very real and very horrible things — at the hands of other agents. In fact, and it pains me to say this, some of the worst things I saw in my career were at the hands of agents. Or maybe it just seemed that way because I didn't expect it. They tarnished the badge, and they tarnished the reputation of the agency with their behavior and for that, I will forever be incredibly disappointed and angry. I will not get into every sordid incident, you can google that stuff, except to give a few specific personal experiences, only one of which Google knows anything about. Here goes.

Fatal Attraction

I had been an agent for about 6 years. I was a new supervisor with only maybe a year under my belt in that position. I was assigned to midnight shift for the entire first year as a supervisor, with a now two-year-old and I desperately wanted to get onto day shift. My husband, also an agent, and I worked opposite shifts throughout our field days, for two reasons: so that our daughter would at least have one parent around most of the time and because he outranked me most of our career. And the agency frowned upon spouses working on the same unit, particularly if one of them outranked the other. This, it turned out, was a wise decision on their part. No one could ever say he favored me, or I favored him because we never worked in a circumstance that brought it into question.

Anyway, I saw an opportunity to put in for the supervisor of the station level training unit. I would report directly to a second level supervisor (we called them Field Operations Supervisors, FOS for short), who was one of the agents that picked up my class to visit the Nogales Station in those first days when we entered on duty, approximately 6 years earlier. He had been over the training unit for some time and was trusted wholeheartedly with its running. He knew who I was because I was also a certified Field Training Officer (FTO) before being promoted, and worked for him in that capacity on the Field Training Unit. He was one of the FOSs on my midnight shift, though not my rating supervisor. We had worked around each other, but not close together up to this point. To protect the not so innocent, I'll call him fatal attraction.

As time progressed, and as all supervisors in my position previously did, I would go out to the field with him on occasion, on hikes, to check on trails, keep up our field skills to not forget the area and mindfully catalog any changes over time. He was my partner those days.

When you ride with someone, a partner, you talk. You talk about yourselves, your lives, and your experiences. You get to know each other. In some circumstances, partners become family. In the Border Patrol, however, you could have a different partner every shift, so it was a different scenario having the same partner most days. I remember sharing quite a bit about my mom and growing up as I did. My mom had recently passed so I spoke about my life, taking care of her and so on.

People generally have an opinion of me from what they see on the surface, but once they get to know me, suffice it to say, I have layers. I had/have a particular look and I don't typically give much away unless I know you—I have the most epic RBF (resting bitch face). I've been told many times that I am very stoic, even aloof.

That is the person he knew.

One day in particular, I finally realized something was different about the way he treated me. We were out in the field, and he pulled the truck over, picked a wildflower and gave it to me. I thought that was weird. I'm not always that quick on the uptake of human behavior of a certain flavor. I typically have no idea if someone is flirting with me. I said thank you and put it on the dash of the truck where it shriveled and died in the desert sun by the time we were done for the day.

At some point, I realized he wasn't allowing me to pay for lunch. One time, no biggie, ok, I'll get it next time. Two times, hmm, he's just being nice. The third time — well, *I am a trained observer* — this wasn't normal.

Sometime later, he came by my office and said "Hey, let's head out to the field." Ok, I guess so, but by this time, I felt a little uneasy about being alone with him. My "trained observer" senses were kicking in. I didn't feel like I had a choice though. He always drove. We ended up way back in a canyon, where no one would likely come upon us. This wasn't terribly unusual; we had hiked some pretty remote places before. He stopped the truck, put it in park, and I thought, ok, we are going on a hike, so I grabbed my hat and exited the vehicle.

As I got out of the truck, he was directly in front of me with this creepy, dopey, lovesick grin on his face.

Shit!

I closed my door and crossed my arms in a clear, come no further stance. I couldn't breathe and I was not sure what the hell was about to happen. He was not reading my body language and approached me as if to try and kiss me, attempting to put his arms on either side of me as I backed up and bumped into the side of the truck. I put my arm straight out and shoved him on the chest. Physically. Pushed. Him. Away.

He was dejected and confused, I guess. I told him, NO, absolutely not, and to take me back to the station immediately. He apologized profusely. I don't remember the drive back, but I don't think we spoke. I could not even turn and look at him. As I type this story, my anxiety shoots through the roof as if I am there in that moment and the terrible feeling of being trapped. Thank God, he didn't push it any further.

What signs were I giving this guy that made him think this was going to happen? Because I had to have done something or said something to provoke this, right? I didn't know how to set boundaries without being a bitch or thought of as a bitch. I didn't want that.

Think about that for just a minute. I was one of 3% in the entirety of the patrol. and I'm the *only* female assigned to this unit at that time. I am a unicorn. This is how women were seen: you're one of the guys, you're a lesbian, or you're just a straight-up bitch. If you're one of the guys, you just let things slide. If you turn someone down or you're not "sweet" to them, you must be a lesbian, or a bitch, or both. Typing that makes me want to vomit. I hate people.

I don't remember why, but for some reason Fatal Attraction took a few midnight shifts, maybe to cover someone on leave or earn overtime. Nonetheless, he was gone for a few days.

However, he started calling me. When he was off duty, at my office, leaving messages, apparently drunk, in the middle of the day professing his love for me. I would tell him; you have to stop. He didn't get the message.

This was my boss, my superior. What can I do or say here? If I say or do the wrong thing, how would that impact me, my career,

41

my marriage? He was well-known and well-respected around the station. Would anyone even believe me?

I know what advice I would give someone else in that situation, but it is not so easy when you are the victim. I didn't tell anyone what was going on. If I filed an EEO complaint—I would be "that girl" and the black cloud would follow me for the rest of my career. I couldn't sleep. I started calling in sick to work and I finally realized that I could not handle this myself. I confessed to my husband what was going on. He asked, "Why didn't you tell me sooner?" I said, "I was trying to handle it myself and I need your help now." Not so funny coincidence, my husband shared an office with this dude. He had known him since his career started, some 8-10 years ago.

My husband confronted Fatal Attraction and very clearly warned him to stay away from me. Fatal Attraction took his time getting that message. He came by my office shortly thereafter and when I saw him approaching, besides that immediate fight or flight reaction in my gut, I was thinking, "What the fuck, dude? My husband is going to murder you."

He came in and closed the door. I could not get far enough away from him. It was a small office with two desks already taking up most of the space. He sat down at the desk not two feet from me and proceeded to ask, "Why did you tell your husband?"

I said, "I told you to stop all the time and you were not hearing me." I told him I wasn't sleeping; I didn't want to come to work, etc. At this very moment, I think a light bulb went off for him.

He finally got it, he turned bright red, apologized, and said, "You did tell me to stop," and excused himself from my space. I ran into him several years later after having left the station and still got that creepy vibe...*shiver*...

Don't Text Me

Fast forward about 7 years and two moves later, around 2012-13, I was assigned to the Rio Grande Valley Sector. There, I was running a sector-wide team dedicated to arresting and convicting transnational criminal organizations—sounds super high-speed, right? My title at this time was Assistant Chief Patrol Agent, a second-level supervisory position. I supervised supervisors; there were approximately 5 or so of us in the Sector. Anyway, I had a first-line supervisor who worked for me running the tactical team—the folks who were going to put their hands on the bad guys and take them to jail. He was kind to me, respectful, did what was asked of him, and by all accounts, he was a good agent. He was a supervisor that worked on my shift a few years earlier when I was his FOS.

As time went on, I developed what I thought was a solid work-relationship with this guy. He came to me with personal problems, we chatted off and on, we worked well together, and I respected him and his work ethic. I have this habit of giving nicknames to people. He had a nickname. It wasn't really a nickname; I just pronounced his name incorrectly. Apparently, that meant I wanted to sleep with him.

One day, seemingly out of the blue, he solicited me to have an affair with him via text on my work phone. At first, I thought this was a joke. He couldn't be serious. I responded, "No thank you, I'm happily married." He said, "So am I."

What the actual FUCK? This came out of nowhere. I saw no signs. I pushed him off and tried to ignore it, but he continued for days. I politely told him no, it was not going to happen, and I was not interested. At this point, I had grown into a pretty confident person, and I did not have time for this horseshit. No means no, dude. I was under a lot of pressure to get this unit on track and functioning. I was trying to figure out how to just make him stop. But I was hesitant, as this was my work phone, and I didn't want to hurt his feelings. Why in the hell did I care about his feelings?

Finally, I very plainly told him, via text, "Do not text me again unless it has to do with work." I thought, if nothing else, I have evidence of the conversation if he ever tried to come back at me for any reason. He apologized, probably half-afraid I would report him, but that was the end of that.

I thought, Jeezus, you can't even be nice to people without them thinking you want to sleep with them.

I started getting a picture now. I was learning lessons about myself, and others. I was becoming more guarded, more direct. You never really know people — I mean, it took me 18 years to realize it at this point. But this place is full of these dudes. Maybe it is kind of rape-y.

The Border Patrol Peeper

I saved the worst for last, the crème de la crème.

Another move and several years later, probably in 2014 or 2015. I was still an Assistant Chief Patrol Agent, but in the San Diego Sector, assigned as the lead for the sector-wide Professional Standards Program. This included a team of agents who were trained to respond to critical incidents.

The Supervisor over the team, a tenured agent, who had overseen this team for probably 5 years by this time came to my office one morning. It was odd, in the first place, that he was even there. His office was miles away on another compound and he did not come to the Sector unless called upon to do so.

It was even odder that he was milling about outside my office as I came out of the conference room after the morning staff meeting.

We did not have a meeting scheduled so I was taken aback by his presence. He asked if he could speak to me in private, so we went into my office, and I closed the door. He sat down in front of me, my desk between us, and proceeded to tell me the following story:

He started by saying that the "Girls found a camera in the women's restroom at his office location and had taken it downtown to the Office of Professional Responsibility (OPR)." OPR is Internal Affairs but for the government. OPR is not part of the Border Patrol but of our parent agency, Customs and Border Protection (CBP).

Ok, he had my attention.

"What do you mean they found a camera?" I asked. He proceeded to explain that he suspected one of the girls, as he referred to the women on his team, was doing drugs at the office and put a camera in the women's restroom to try and catch her. I asked him why he thought she may be doing drugs. He could only say that she was moody and dismissive. This in my mind was no indication of drug use.

This team was made up of 95% women — not normal for any team in the USBP. I realized at this moment that I needed a witness to this conversation. Every single hair on the back of my neck was on end, because this guy was full of shit. I told him to stand by and I went to find someone to come into my office to hear this. I could only find my Deputy Chief. The man was essentially in charge of the entire Sector.

I told him that I needed a witness, briefly described the story so far, and asked if he would come with me. He knew me well, we had worked in the field together years before in Nogales, so he knew when I was serious. Intrigued and concerned, he followed. I told this agent to tell the story again, which he did. I also realized that I should not ask too many questions because I did not want to risk a future investigation.

So, I listened to him tell the same BS story once again.

I grew angry. I grew upset. I wanted to reach across the desk and ring his ugly disgusting neck. He was *creeping me out*.

The reality of the situation was that this guy was a voyeur, a peeping Tom. The headlines would read, "Border Patrol Peeper..."

He'd put a camera in the drain just below the toilet and angled it to take X-rated photos of anyone who used that restroom. The "girls" found the camera because they caught him coming out of the women's restroom. He made some excuse that he was fixing a leak — which they would have known about if there were one. They found a screwdriver in the medicine chest, and being trained investigators themselves, found the little camera in the drain. After multiple conversations with the local police and the two internal affairs investigative agencies for both DHS and CBP, I and another female agent, along with one of the investigators, proceeded to search this agent's office. What we found was nothing less than vile.

Inside a seemingly harmless and benign coffee mug — the insulated kind of tumbler with the clear plastic top that is so popular these days — was a tiny little SD card. A memory card and something like $5,000 cash. On that memory card were at least two years' worth of graphic pictures of women, in what could be argued were their most private moments. I didn't even want to know what the cash was about. Are you fucking serious? What is wrong with people?

Why don't we do psychological exams before we hire people? This was not the first time I asked that question, or the last.

I ended up testifying before the Grand Jury. He was indicted on the only charge that we could find that carried any consequence – lying to a federal officer. When he lied to me and told me he placed the camera in that restroom to try and catch one of his employees doing drugs – he'd sealed his fate.

Unfortunately, there was no federal charge for voyeurism and the state charges carried less of a penalty than the federal lying charge, so the US Attorney's office, in conjunction with state and local authorities, chose to pursue the charge with the stiffer penalty. It was only a year in jail, but it was more than a fine and a walk. He was eventually convicted.

It turned out that he, and he alone, selected the agents on this team, and he selected mostly women – pretty, young female agents.

My co-worker had the horrible task of having to look at all the pictures in an attempt to identify all of the victims. I cannot imagine the damage that did to her psyche. She did it out of obligation to those who were victimized. She is an amazing person. We bonded over rescuing border dogs and our love of fluffy creatures – sound familiar? Different female, same commonality.

Chapter 6
Border Dogs: The Healing Power of the Fluff!

For the love of dogs!

Ok, enough heavy stuff for now. Let's talk about something good. DOGS!

My love for dogs began as a child, probably since birth. I cannot remember a time when I did not have, at minimum, one dog in my life. I don't have much of a preference: big, small, long-haired, short-haired, heavy, light, fluffy, matted — I don't care. I will go into any dark, dingy, scary place regardless of any signs of danger just to pet a dog, or rescue one. I don't care much what people think of me, but I am completely dejected if a dog won't let me pet it. In fact, the only people I like to meet anymore are DOGS.

Also, dogs don't judge. They are excited to see you no matter what you do. They expect the bare minimum from you: food, water, and a spot next to you on the couch. My dog also expects treats every time he comes in from outside, and a little help getting up on the couch. And by GOD, he deserves it all. Dogs don't hold grudges; they shit and kick dirt on it, that is how we all should handle the shit in our lives. Everyone who knows me knows and understands that dogs make up the fabric of my being.

Circa 1999, maybe 2000, Kathy — the agent who was 100-star numbers behind me — and I were partnered up for the day. We were assigned "east side rover" a highly coveted assignment typically reserved for the hard-working agents who knew the area well, and could be trusted to be anywhere and respond to just about anything. It meant we had an immense amount of autonomy to work just about any traffic we chose. This day wasn't terribly busy. We had responded to a few sensor hits and were checking out the area around a house where illegal aliens [this is my story, and I will be using words that are just fucking words—don't flake out and get offended. They are legal terms in the law] were known to lay up and wait for their smuggler to pick them up.

As we approached the house, we noticed a fluffy brown, white, and black, medium to large-sized dog lying on the porch, maybe a border collie mix of some kind. He didn't move much, barely lifted his head to look at us. He was clearly not a threat. We didn't think that this was his house, verified later by the owner of the home—or maybe they saw an opportunity to get him some help. As we got closer, he slowly got up and started to amble toward us.

As he approached, this putrid smell of what I can only describe as dead, rotting flesh, wafted over both of us. We quickly noticed that one of his ears was literally hanging from the top of his head, matted with blood and by the smell, it was severely infected. Coyotes probably got to him, poor guy. He was so sweet and came right up to us as if to ask for help. I had two dogs at home, in my two-bedroom apartment, one of which was a border rescue, and I could not bring home another one or I risked divorce.

Probably not really, but I was fairly new at the marriage thing and didn't want to push my luck. As the years passed, my husband has come to realize that he doesn't have a choice. When it comes to dogs, I'm going to do what I'm going to do.

Nearby, there was a shelter that offered veterinary services. We decided to take him there. I explained that we had just found him, and he desperately needed medical treatment. The staff were very accommodating. I told them that I would pay whatever the cost was to fix him up, but I could not take him home with me. They agreed to help. I paid with a credit card and if my husband is reading this, he now knows, because I never told him this, but I doubt he is surprised.

Several days, maybe a week later, when assigned to that area again, I stopped in the shelter to check on our injured friend. There he was, all sewn up, sans the infected, putrid ear and instead 15 staples across his shaved head where his ear used to be. He was so happy to see me, and I probably cried a little, maybe one tear, seeing him this way. He was clearly feeling better. The staff told me that they had an adopter interested in him, one of the staff, in fact. I cannot tell you the relief that gave me. I would have taken this dog home if no one showed interest, but I honestly did not want to do that to my husband, or my other dogs.

They dubbed him Frankenstein, Franky for short, a perfect name for this border rescue. Happy ending! Dogs are the best.

There are hundreds of border dogs living, mostly wild, along the entire border of the US and Mexico. Some are dumped, some are born out there, and some wander across the border from Mexico. Border towns are not typically thriving metropolises. The people live in extreme poverty and many barely have the means to survive. Most areas along the southern border in the US are ranches, and not a lot of homes or people live right along the border, except for the western side of the San Diego Sector, along the Pacific Coast—in particular where Tijuana, Baja California, and San Ysidro, CA meet.

Of all the places I worked and lived, San Diego was by far the biggest city. It was also where I was the most involved and saw the worst of the border dog situation.

As I mentioned previously, I want to pet ALL the dogs. Border dogs are mostly wild, feral, and very distrustful of humans. However, they are also hungry and thirsty. They didn't want to be pets, or they didn't yet know they wanted to be pets — that's what I like to believe.

The feral border dogs would see the white SUVs that agents drove around in and know that most agents would share at least a nibble from their lunch with them. They would very carefully approach the trucks and wait for some tasty morsel to be thrown from the window. The vehicles weren't a threat.

In my work truck, I would carry my "dog rescue kit." Just in case I came upon a stray dog sometime during my shift. Canned dog food, a water jug full of water, a bowl, a leash, and turkey jerky. They couldn't resist the stuff.

Jenny

Jenny started as a stray, down by the border in San Diego, not too far from the beach near Imperial Beach, CA. She was a fluffy brown Australian Shepard mix with light brown eyes. Border dogs always have the prettiest eyes. She was hanging out around an area where agents sat in a static position, watching the border. Smart girl. She would get food and water and safety around those white SUVs.

I worked with a rescue while living in California called Rescuing Cujo that — a retired FBI agent started up when he retired. I would contact him for help or advice whenever there was a dog I was going to try to get off the border. Jenny didn't belong there since she wasn't wild, so someone had to have dumped her. Rescuing Cujo would take her if I could catch her. She was, come to find out, incredibly fearful. I couldn't get near her.

I spoke with the agents who worked in that area. At the time, I was the commander of the Imperial Beach station, so they all worked for me, technically. I came to find out they were trying to trap her, as well.

Agents can be the most compassionate people you will ever meet. There are too many to count that have taken home border dogs over the years—and these dogs will make the best pets when given the opportunity.

Long story short, we eventually trapped her with the help of the humane society and took her to the shelter. They wouldn't release her to me from the border, so if I wanted her, I had to go and adopt her. Turned out that was the best scenario for Jenny. I would go and visit her at the shelter on the weekends, bringing my portable kennel and leash every time, ready to take her home with me.

One problem: she was the most fearful dog I had ever seen. A fearful dog will shut down and I had no idea how to handle that.

I'd sit by her kennel with "high quality" treats in hand and wait for hours for her to realize I was her friend. High-quality treats include steak that I had cooked up and cut into bite-sized pieces. Steak that I bought for my family (sorry fam). But this dog needed me. I threw the pieces of meat to her between the bars of the kennel and she would move just enough to get one at a time...and immediately retreat to the furthest corner of the kennel she could get to. I visited her for several weeks and I knew that this was not a no-kill shelter, so I was getting very concerned.

I arrived one Saturday morning, kennel in the truck, decision made. She was going home with me, one way or another, and I'd deal with the fearful dog situation. I'd bought a book on the subject and I was ready to accept the challenge. I walked around the shelter, but I couldn't find her—Oh God, was I too late, they said she had more time.

I stopped at the front desk, and they said she was gone.

WHAT?! What do you mean? Her time isn't up yet!

The girl at the desk said, "No, someone picked her up, and adopted her."

WHAT?

"OMG—who, please tell me, I want to contact them."

Turned out, that they couldn't release that information, but they would give my contact information to the adopter. Thank Jesus!

Turned out, Aussie Rescue of San Diego had adopted her. They contacted me and I started following their Facebook page for updates. They named her Jenny!

I watched as she progressed from an incredibly fearful dog to the magical post wherein Jenny was walking on a leash, with a pep in her step, happily accepting treats from the hand of her handler. JOY! RAPTURE! Happy Ending. Dogs are the best.

Stewart

Stewart's Bridge was a landmark within the Imperial Beach station area of responsibility, another static position that all agents knew well. My troops notified me of a friendly border dog was hanging out in the area for some time.

"You have to get him, ma'am, we'll help, he's really sweet," they told me.

Alright, when and where?

Some border dogs have a particular look to them — a breed of their own it seems — and when you see one, you know they are a border dog. Ears just a little too big for their head, standing up on end, very pretty, multi-colored eyes, short hair, typically, and really any mix of color you can think of. They're all a little too skinny, for obvious reasons.

Stewart, named such because he hung out at Stewart's Bridge, was just such a dog. Mostly black, with some white and brown mixed in, those crazy ears, the prettiest color of light brown, maybe you could say hazel, eyes, and a bit of a limp.

I gave the agents my kennel and they set up the trap.

A few days later, one of the ATV agents called me at the office and said, "Ma'am, we got him." I thought they meant a smuggler, but they said, "No, we got Stewart."

Oh my Gosh, even better. Look, I had my priorities!

"We're bringing him to the station now." Oh my — where is my dog rescue kit? He had to be starving. They pulled up with Stewart in the kennel in the bed of the truck and he was just ecstatic. I don't know if he had a single clue what was going on, but he was a goofball. He licked my hand and had this look, like 'I'm just happy to be here.'

I ended up taking Stewart home with me — he was the friendliest guy. My dog didn't appreciate it, but that was ok because we had played this game before. I tried to integrate Stewart into our little pack, but he was clearly not going to be able to be an inside dog. And my bulldog, who had recently become an only dog, was not having it.

This is how it would go, as it had before—I bring home a dog, my dogs don't like it, we rotate the herd when animals need to go out, and they never cross paths. And everyone is happy, except my husband, but Stewart was just a lovable pup. He had probably lived outside his whole life, but it was winter in CA and I lived about 30 miles inland, up toward the mountains where it got cold at night. Freezing cold. We had horse corrals on our property and a tack shed—perfect for housing a stray dog at night with a little space heater to keep him warm.

Stewart was so happy. He was also a free spirit and would not be contained. Not the last rescue with that characteristic. He escaped from the corrals daily, despite my best attempts to fortify them. But he always came back when I arrived home. I thought about renaming him Rocket because when I threw a ball, he would take off like a rocket, hightailing it as fast as he could. I needed to find Stewart his own family though and partnered with my new friend from Rescuing Cujo for some tips and tricks to give Stewart a little training and make him the best dog possible for a new family.

One of the agents from my station ended up taking Stewart. He owed his kids a pup and Stewart was perfect for two young energetic boys to love on. He showed me pictures of the dog house he and his kids built for Stewart. It was perfect. Happy Ending! Dogs are the best.

Betty White

Betty White wasn't a border dog that I rescued from the border. She might have been at some point, but when I rescued her, she was a stray from death row at a kill shelter. Betty White, originally known as Becky, showed up on my Facebook feed one day. I was struggling with anxiety, stress, being overworked, and really wanted to just walk away from the job and never turn back. By now, I was involved with a few rescue organizations while living in San Diego and I followed their Facebook pages. One of them posted a "code red" alert that Becky, a fluffy mix of some type, would be put down in 24 hours if no one adopted her. I could not let that happen.

The rescue organization would pay all her fees and vet bills if someone could foster her. I needed a mental health break, and I needed to do something good. I contacted the rescue organization to say I would take her in, asked them to notify the shelter, and I'd be there in an hour or so.

I called in sick to work and headed to get her.

Once I showed up at the shelter, I hung around in the courtyard area for a bit with Becky so that I could see how she would react. She wouldn't come near me. Another fearful dog. By this time, I figured I could handle it. I would take some time off, find out what she needed, and we would get through it. It was only a temporary situation. If a foster keeps a dog they have fostered, it's called a foster failure. I didn't want to be a failure, so I was not going to end up keeping her. I was able to hand over the cutest puppy I had fostered earlier in the year to her forever family, surely, I could do this.

Becky was a fluffy blonde girl—probably a husky mix, according to the vet. She desperately needed a good bath and brushing. I later renamed her Betty White because of her white/blonde hair, and the fact she was 11 years old, an old lady in dog years. Seemed perfect.

She allowed me to put a leash on her and I got her into my jeep. She spent the entire hour-and-a-half drive standing on the middle console, panting, whining, and drooling right next to my face while looking out the front window. She did not settle at all. She would let me pet her and licked my face a few times. I thought she was going to be just fine. Turned out, this was how she would always behave on car rides.

At the house, she searched around a bit, sniffed my bulldog, and sat herself down as far as she could get from me. I didn't know if she had ever been in a house, and if she had, she likely hadn't been allowed on furniture. I would offer for her to come and sit next to me on the couch, but she just looked at me from across the room and her eyes said, "You can't fool me, I'm not coming up there." She wouldn't even lay at my feet.

She was very well-behaved and never had an accident in the house even once. She didn't chew on anything, but she HATED to be detained or restrained in a kennel. She always settled across the room, where I think she could keep an eye on things, her back to the wall. The only time she responded was to go outside, and I had to leash her up or she would take off like a bat out of hell.

I spent a lot of time sat in the middle of the floor, just wait to see if she would come and check me out. She eventually came around, and would let me pet her. She was initially very scared to turn her back to me, or Sandler, my bulldog. Sandler was ok with Betty White. I think because she kept her distance from his human. I would have to stand behind her while she ate inside the pantry, because she needed to feel safe and have privacy. And Sandler would absolutely steal her food.

Betty White loved to be outside, walking, running, chasing rabbits and sniffing. Given even the smallest opportunity, she would take off running. On one occasion, one of my coworkers was dog-sitting while I was out of town on a work trip. She had to take the dogs out and made the mistake of opening the door before she had the leash on Betty White.

Sandler, the bulldog wasn't taking off running for nothing. But Betty White only needed a sliver of light and freedom to take her opportunity and that was exactly what she did. My colleague would tell me how she ran all over our 2 acres chasing Betty White; oops, I forgot to tell her not to chase Betty White and just wait for her to come back. She always came back. My coworker eventually got her, and all ended well. Lesson learned.

I had rescued Betty White sometime in July. That fall, I was beginning to apply for jobs back east, at HQ in Washington, DC. I received an offer for a position in October and I had to report the first week of December.

We were in the midst of selling our home and preparing for the move. Whenever someone wanted to see the house, we would get the dogs out and take a walk or a drive. However, I lived about 30 miles from where I worked, so if someone wanted to view the house in the middle of the day, I couldn't just get the dogs out. They had to be in kennels.

Sandler was crate-trained and had no issue. Betty White on the other hand…

I came home one day after work, having put her in the kennel before I left that morning. Simply giving it a try. What I came home to was the kennel turned upside down, bent, bitten, crunched and her outside it. Ok, then.

The rescue organization had been relatively quiet and did not seem to be attempting to find a forever home for her. I contacted them to make it clear that they had to find her a home or another foster *before* Thanksgiving.

I'd had Betty White for four months by this time. We had sold our house and were moving across the country in a matter of weeks.

The rescue finally came through and she would go to a home on a ranch. However, I was in the process of moving, and they needed to meet at a particular location to pick her up. My husband would have to do the drop off.

She had eventually come around to both my daughter and me...and then my husband came home from a long-term detail. She was terrified of him.

Betty White would not allow him to put the leash on her. I had to take her out or do anything that involved getting close to her. It would take another few months before she would allow him to come near her. She would do so on her own, on occasion, at first just to let him take her out. She finally softened toward him.

Just as my husband had gained her trust, he was the one to take her to a stranger and put her in their van. UGH. Nevertheless, Betty White found her forever home on a ranch with other dogs where she could run to her heart's delight and be free.

It was always hard to give up a dog after fostering them, but I knew they were going to good homes, so that lightened the load. Happy Ending. Dogs are the best.

The other agents and I rescued dogs all over the place. We took them out of drainpipes, abandoned houses, and yards in Mexico, particularly puppies, I mean, we didn't go into Mexico, but the dogs did cross the border to us. Agents would snatch them up and find them homes.

Remember my co-worker who had to view all those awful pictures to identify victims of the peeper? She single-handedly rescued hundreds of border dogs throughout her career. This is primarily what she was known for, and she continued the practice into her retirement. Everyone called her when they came across a stray. She is a saint.

Insight into the power of an animal on the human psyche.

I think that when you see the ugliest things that society and the world have to offer, people generally just want to do something good and make a difference. For an animal, for their family, and for their community. When you are exposed to the worst in humanity, rescuing and loving a dog, or any animal, can provide a type of healing that I can't even explain. It is just a good deed, pure and simple. When I was at the worst point in my career, mentally — stressed, depressed, and suffering from PTSD, I'd take leave and go rescue a dog.

I wasn't the only person suffering. The agency had suffered multiple suicides and some of the worst press you could receive. The border was out of control and agents could only do so much. We were in the spotlight, and bad news always gets more attention than good news. Agents were vilified, condemned, called Nazis. It was disgusting behavior.

When people are under stress, they tend to self-medicate — alcohol, drugs, bad behavior. The agency was involved in the Portland riots, the DC riots, the school shooting in Uvalde, TX, and every mass border incursion in the last 100 years. Agents were suffering at a level never seen before.

We needed to do something different to combat this. Things needed to change.

Well…

What if we had an office dog?

I mean, seriously, what if the Border Patrol had a program where dogs provide support to our agents and employees?

I used to bring my bulldog to the office every now and then when I was the commander of a station. Usually on a Friday, along with a pan of brownies. Brownie Friday! It was my station; I did what I wanted (wink).

What I started to notice was that people would come by more often. They wanted to see Sandler. And they wanted a brownie.

"Is Sandler here today?" "Where's Sandler, why didn't you bring him?" "Did she bring brownies today?" The agents would call up to the front office to ask.

Legal disclosure for any ethics lawyers reading this – I never transported Sandler in my government vehicle. Plus, you'd have to drag me out of retirement to punish me.

Critical Incident Response Canine (Support K-9/SK9)

Around 2022, I finally made it through the ranks to a position where I could, at a minimum, influence and make decisions for programs and policies that could have positive impacts on the agency and the employees. I had left the uniform and the badge a few years earlier, taking a promotion into a senior executive position outside of law enforcement, leaving the Border Patrol.

I did that for about 18 months and then after experiencing what it was like to work for a true misogynist, had the opportunity to return to the USBP in a senior executive position as a civilian. I took over the role of Executive Director for the National-Level Mission Support Directorate, which oversaw all of the agency's wellness and resiliency programs, among a number of other program areas, but this was where my heart was.

For the government, SES is as high as you can go—Senior Executive Service (SES). There are levels of SES, my bosses and peers were also SES. There are a million of them in the Washington, DC area. Ok, maybe not a million. I don't want to give the impression that I ran the agency or anything. Becoming an SES is a difficult path and something I never sought as a goal but am proud of. I couldn't spell SES, much less see myself at that level for most of my career.

After experiencing and dealing with death and despair—line of duty deaths, suicides, deaths of people in our custody, my own personal tragedies—it was a time when the agency was at a turning point.

CBP had something like 16 suicides in one year, the majority of which were Border Patrol Agents, and supervisors at that. Things were bad. I wanted to do something tangible, good, and helpful.

You can only take so many 2 a.m. phone calls before it starts to eat away at your very soul. No good news comes at 2 a.m. The call from the hospital when my mother passed came at 2 a.m. *Sigh.*

I wanted to provide a resource for our employees that they could literally touch, feel, lean on, and hang on. I'm not particularly known for showing my feelings, at least not publicly—most people who only know me on the surface would say I'm direct, not afraid to say what everyone else is thinking.

I'm sarcastic. I like dogs more than people—and if I do say so myself, I'm flippin' hilarious. I have that epic RBF, you know. I can and have handled a lot of shit in my life and when once asked, after having received news of an agent's suicide, "How do you do it?" —

I just said, "I don't know, things have to get done, get taken care of, I have responsibilities. I just push through, I'll cry later."

There was nothing more important to me—as my career progressed, as I matured and experienced some of life's shit that I couldn't just kick dirt over—than *the people*. The people who make up the agency. The people who face danger and criticism for every action or decision they make. The people who take care of the agents—the caregivers, the professional staff. You cannot accomplish the mission without the people.

The agency has robust peer support and chaplaincy functions— one of, if not the best and most mature programs in the federal government. These folks are often asked to train others and assist in standing up other agencies' peer support and chaplaincy programs. The USBP, as a whole, is very good at crisis response, both operationally and behind the scenes. However, we are an agency of type A, 'I always have my shit together,' personalities. We don't cry. We don't have feelings. We don't ask for help. We don't talk about our problems. We are hard, macho, tough and seasoned individuals. We don't tell our spouses or family members what goes on at work, even if they ask.

We Don't Cry—but sometimes our eyes sweat.

However, you put a dog or a puppy in front of most people, people with a proclivity toward helping others, and they soften. I have seen it. Sometimes people have to see it to believe it. They pet the dog; they start talking to whoever is handling the dog. The shell starts to crack a bit.

Lightbulb

I have an idea.

To give credit where credit is due, this was not my idea entirely. My work BFF, Dy and I had talked about something like this for years. In fact, her sector was doing it already—by proxy. An agent, also a veteran—of which we have many—had a service K-9 that he had received as part of some program for veterans. He was working in a capacity at the time that allowed him to bring the pup to work with him. He was also a chaplain.

Agents and other employees sought him out for his chaplaincy expertise and the pup would be there as well. Everyone loved the dog. The response was overwhelmingly positive. And I was now in a position to officially make it happen for the entire agency.

I approached my Chief—of the US Border Patrol—and told him that I want to set up a Support K-9 program.

This man was a seasoned, experienced, "old patrol" man. He had over 30 years in the agency by this time and had served in the military. I worked for him in the past in south Texas, so he knew mostly what to expect from me.

When I asked for this, he gave me a side-eye. "Support K-9, what is that? I don't know about that."

Ok, hear me out.

"We pair our peer support and Chaplaincy certified agents with emotional support K-9s. When they respond to events or people in need, the K-9 accompanies them. It's a doorway, an opening if you will, for Agents and employees to drop their guard and hopefully, HOPEFULLY, open up. Give those with the skillsets to help an opportunity to do so. It can't be just any agent or person handling the dogs, because the dog is not the key here—I mean, they are—but they aren't. The dog is a tool, one of many, in the toolbox of the caretaker. Most people are familiar with emotional support animals, animals that aid the blind, those with certain medical conditions, and veterans. But this is different. This is not something, come to find out, anyone inside or outside of the law enforcement profession is doing. We are about to blaze a trail."

He was cautious, so I pushed; a lot. I think they call it "leading up" in the leadership courses. He acquiesced. Go time.

Except…hmm.

Funding. Funding is always a problem.

Over the last few years, law enforcement in general has been under immense pressure and scrutiny. Unlike in the 90s, when you had to score 100 to even get an interview, LEO agencies worldwide were, and still are, having a really hard time recruiting people into the law enforcement profession. For many reasons, and not a topic for this book, those in the law enforcement profession were targets. Everything we did was in the news or on YouTube or some other social media platform being judged by the masses. Wrong, right, or indifferent, it's a fact.

This only added onto the daily stress agents and employees were feeling and experiencing. Not just at work, but every life stressor you can imagine as well. Eventually, society, or at least a part of it, started to shift and recognize the suffering of first responders.

Much like soldiers, first responders see things that no human being should ever see or experience and over time, that takes a toll. And much like soldiers, they suck it up and internalize it.

The term "resilient" started to become one of those buzzwords you would see or hear everywhere. We probably came up with our definition of it long after we started using it. It started to be overused, over referenced, and every time an email came out referencing resilience training...DELETE, swipe right, or left, whatever you do to delete something.

Intentions were good and in the right place, but the agency was doing a lot of talking and little action. We must be resilient; we need to provide resources to our employees so that they can deal with their issues.

In that vein, Congress started providing funding to CBP to focus on resiliency programs.

AHA—I know how I'm going to pay for this program.

I convinced my Chief to allow me to move forward with a pilot program and we needed to get these teams fielded as soon as possible. Around this time was just after the Uvalde, TX mass school shooting, where it was Border Patrol Agents who eventually shot and killed the shooter. We were in a desperate time. Other agencies had sent a few emotional support K-9s, though not part of an official program, and a few enforcement K-9 flunkies (too friendly for that work) to Texas after the event. And the Chief firsthand saw the impact they had.

My resiliency team did the leg work, research, and eventually we decided on one non-profit organization in California that trained guide dogs for the blind *and* had dogs and training immediately available. Three dogs were available that were already experienced in emotional support and had been trained specifically for that purpose. Two black lab puppies, about 6 months old, that we could get for half the cost of fully grown, trained dogs. The organization would train the handlers as well in a weeklong certification course.

One week? That's it? Ok, I guess these people know what they're doing.

You see, I was on a time crunch. It was December of 2022 and I was eligible to retire in a year and a few months. And I definitely wanted to retire at that time, at least from the government. To set up a program from start to finish can take up to 3 years or longer.

Ain't nobody got time for that. There was an immediate need.

I begged CBP for the money. In the larger scheme of government budgets, I was asking for pennies. Congress had allocated about $25 million in appropriated funding to CBP for its resiliency programs. CBP was looking at setting up a new directorate and attempting to hire field psychologists and clinicians, so $25 million wouldn't go far. However, I was only asking for around $60,000. This would pay for five dogs, the training and the travel for five handlers. I provided the research, the facts, the cost, pictures of the dogs—surely, you can't say no after seeing these photos of the puppies and a standard poodle named Chappie.

Excuse me—Chappie? Oh Lord, what are we doing? We are going to need to change that name…and a poodle…I don't know.

In fact, all the dogs' names were well, just not cool. What would people think? Pearl, Chappie, Janet, Gene and Jackie—ok, what is with all the J sounding names? And why so old fashioned? Two yellow labs (Pearl and Jackie), two black labs (Gene and Janet— brother and sister puppies), and one gray, curly topped standard poodle. And HIS FUCKING NAME IS CHAPPIE.

Generally, USBP dogs were Belgian Malinois or some kind of high drive Shepard. Crazy, hard-wired working dogs, sourced and trained in Germany or someplace like that. Their commands were in

German, which just sounds harsh to begin with. And their names suited them—Dutch, Rex, Killer, I-Will-Tear-Your-Face-Off. (maybe not those last two). They bite their handlers and it's expected to happen. On occasion, the handlers will get to a point with some of these dogs where they have to Alpha roll them. They literally roll around on the ground with the dog to gain control and show them the human is the alpha in that relationship.

You get what I'm saying? This program was just about as opposite as you can get from that.

My team and I hand selected the top 5 best and most active peer support and chaplaincy certified individuals. Agents that we knew would work hard and do their best to make this program a success. They had already proven themselves as some of the best peer support and chaplaincy representatives.

There were a lot of unknowns and things we didn't know to consider at the beginning. But if we started with the best teams possible, success would surely come.

We only renamed one of the dogs. Gene became Blitzen— named so in honor of one of our biggest supporters whose black lab, Blitzen, had recently passed. Upon finding out Janet meant "God's gracious gift," we couldn't change her name. And Pearl just fit—a plump older lady with perfect manners who has kisses for everyone she met. Jackie wasn't so bad to begin with, lucky girl. Chappie kept his name. Turns out, it's perfect for him.

Chappie, once shunned for his uppity name and appearance, was by far the most popular support K-9. (I love you all the same, Janet, Blitzen, Jackie, Pearl and Chappie—but facts are facts). Chappie stood out—he was a tall, distinguished gentleman poodle who wore a bow tie, for the love of Pete. Perfect! Absolutely contrary to anything you think of when you think of the Border Patrol.

All the dogs became very popular in the Sectors where they were assigned, not just within the agency, but throughout their communities. The handlers were referred to by their dog's name — Janet's mommy, Chappie's Daddy. Sorry guys and girls, you were just a body at the other end of the leash. The dogs were greeted first and if someone remembered, they eventually said hello to the handler with a, "What's your name, again?"

I kid, I kid. The handlers were, in fact, the most important part of the equation.

We added a sixth dog, Arthur, shortly thereafter, and I loved him too. He was the lady's man. Jackie was his favorite girl.

In January of 2023, the program went live. All six of the agents and the dogs passed the certification and they were off to do God's work, if you will. We developed policies and procedures, largely based on the already existing enforcement K-9 program.

The concept was simple — when called upon, the agent would respond to a crisis situation, either on the border or to an employee in crisis — any situation you can think of where someone may need a Chaplain or Peer Support, the canine would accompany them. Dogs are used in therapeutic situations all the time. Counseling, court testimony, hospital and retirement home visits, school programs, you name it. The idea was that the dog was a mechanism to get folks to become more comfortable and unload some of their burdens, and at a minimum start to recognize or ask for help — or just be present to support someone in crisis or suffering.

The reception of the program was mixed initially. Both internal and external to the agency, people had opinions.

Retired agents felt like they still had a say, and they would contact current leadership to share their opinions, or they would put them all over social media. The reception by some in the retirement community as well as current agents was nasty, unrelenting, old patrol negativity. As the program rolled out, the agency put out a news release. It didn't take long for any kind of word or rumor to spread in this agency. Biddies in the barber shop kind of gossipers.

If you want any kind of information to make its way far and wide, you just tell a Border Patrol Agent. Everyone will know in a matter of hours.

Add to that, the advent of social media. Lord, have mercy on my soul! Comments such as "What has happened to my beloved patrol – you're all a bunch of weak pu$$!3$."

It was disheartening, disappointing, uneducated, uninformed, and cruel. I don't know why I subject myself to the comment section, but I always do. Fuck those guys.

By and large, however, the reception turned out to be overwhelmingly positive. It was interesting to see that once the positive comments and experiences started becoming known, the detractors and Negative Nancy's seemed to disappear.

Once people started seeing the impact of the handlers and the canines, they requested them for everything. Parades, school events, critical incidents, shootings, funerals, family tragedies, family days, and so on. Not just some events. *ALL* the events.

Six handlers (human beings with lives and issues of their own) responded to events around the nation, non-stop in addition to making their required rounds to every station within their assigned sectors. The peer support and chaplain agents didn't say no. They stepped up and responded. Sector leadership began to treat them as if they were mascots and the only resiliency resource they had. That was never the intent.

This was something we didn't anticipate — the demand, the overwhelming demand.

We had to re-adjust a year into the program. We needed to provide the handlers with a mechanism to say no, i.e. writing mandatory down-time into the policy to set the sector leadership straight on the intent of the program. (*Sector Chiefs LOVE being told they can't do something, insert sarcasm font.*) And we also needed to expand the resource and deploy more teams.

The second year of the program would be a year of refinement and expansion. It was now January 2024. More now than ever, I was feeling the pressure to set it all straight, get it all right, in accordance with my vision for the program before my departure. This was my program, my baby, my crowning achievement. I really could care less if I accomplished anything else for the organization.

I did the best I could to set the stage before my departure. I would have to trust that the powers that be continued the program the way it is meant to be. There were four additional pups purchased and as I type, they and their handlers just graduated to go on to become the next set of Critical Incident Response (CIR) Canines.

It was my time to go when the sun set and start my next chapter in life. During my retirement send off, the canine team bestowed upon me a gift that really touched my heart. While we were away as a team, reviewing the program for the first year, we had the opportunity to have professional photos of the handlers and their K-

9 partners. During this photoshoot, I also had the chance to get a photo with all six of my furry babies, seated on the ground amongst them, grinning from ear to ear.

The team dubbed me "Mother of SK9s," similar to the popular HBO series, *Game of Thrones'* Daenerys Tygaryen and her dragons — the Mother of Dragons. Also, they gifted me with a plaque with said photo with the dogs and paw prints etched into the wood with their names.

Chapter 7
Field Stories

I know I'm all over the place, timeline wise, so I'm going to attempt to take you on a more sensical journey.

I attended a leadership training not-so-long ago, during which they taught a lesson about storytelling. The power of a story – when told properly and at the right time. I tell stories when something makes me remember them, when I'm wrapped up in a conversation with someone and I get a jolt of a memory – "Oh, I have story." I tell some stories over and over again, as they are good lessons in leadership. Some stories are just funny, and others are life lessons.

When I came into the USBP in 1996, traffic on the southern border was very busy. San Diego Sector was the hot spot in the early to mid-1990's, with kamikaze runs through the San Ysidro Port of Entry and no border infrastructure. People just making a run for it, probably hundreds at a time, maybe more. The USBP didn't have many cameras along the border, so it was hard to say outside of agent accounts, how many people crossed the border at a time. When I graduated from the academy and arrived in Nogales, the traffic was starting to shift to Arizona, throughout the Tucson Sector.

Not just human traffic, but drug traffic as well. The USBP began sitting agents in vehicles, nearly hand to hand, along the border in San Diego in what became affectionally known as X's. An agent sat on their X – a static position – not too far from the next agent over, in an effort to tighten up the border. No one wanted to sit X's.

Once San Diego seemed to slow down, Arizona picked up. In order to deal with the uptick in traffic, the agency began sending agents from San Diego, in particular, to Tucson to assist with manpower shortages. It was a good time to be an agent in Nogales. When the detailers came in, the younger agents were given the opportunity to work the more exciting, further out traffic. That was where the large loads of drugs were smuggled across the border.

My First Dope Load

As a trainee, agents were assigned to a training officer — we called them Journeymen in the Border Patrol. My first Journeyman was a seasoned man with white hair and a pretty funny personality. We were assigned checkpoint duties as one of our assignments for the two weeks I was partnered with him. We learned a little about checkpoint duties in the academy, including bus checks. When a bus approaches the checkpoint, which is situated less than 50 miles from the border, there is a higher than likely chance that someone on that bus is out of status, has entered illegally, or is traveling beyond their allowed distance from the border on a visitor visa. One of our lessons was to check the baggage area of the bus and feel the luggage from the outside, to see if it was soft — like clothing. If it wasn't, it was possible there were bricks of drugs inside.

I was brand new, wearing my Elmer Fudd hat, as all trainees were required to wear their cover when in the field, and a bus came to the checkpoint. I was working in secondary, where they sent vehicles that were determined to need a little advanced check. Buses and conveyances that carried multiple occupants were always sent to secondary.

As the bus pulled up and the driver stepped down to open the baggage area — they knew the drill — I approached the bus. I started looking underneath, in the baggage area and feeling each piece of luggage and HOLY CRAP—this one felt different. A teal blue duffel bag. It was definitely not clothing. Oh My God. OH MY GOD. Now I had to find out whose bag it was. No name tag or claim check was attached.

I stepped up onto the bus, duffel in hand, nervous and shaking and held it in the air to ask if it belonged to anyone. Of course, no one answered. Since it was now abandoned, I took it into the secondary area and proceeded to open it.

JACKPOT—several bricks of compacted marijuana. MY FIRST DOPE LOAD.

It weighed maybe 40 pounds. 40 pounds of marijuana. POUNDS. Most street cops get ounces in their entire career. Border Patrol Agents seized pounds, hundreds of pounds, in one seizure. I have a polaroid picture in a worn-out little picture album of me and my first dope load, and my second, and my third…and so on.

"Abandoned" drugs were pretty common throughout the border area. Not because someone left it out there and forgot about it—but this was how the game was played. The smugglers—or mules as we called them—usually men (never met a female doing this), trekked bundles of drugs across the desert on their backs, mostly during the hours of darkness. They would cross the border, be detected in some fashion and agents would then set up to interdict the mules and seize the drugs. Agents performed lay-in operations wherein, since we knew the area well, having walked the smuggling trails during day shift to learn the area and where the mules were likely to come to. Somewhere on a trail in a canyon, in the middle of nowhere, we would sit in the darkness and wait for them to approach. Once the timing was right, agents "jumped" the group. What that means is that you popped up, flashlights on and yelled

"U.S. BORDER PATROL, FREEZE" — but in Spanish — "PARATE."
Mules rarely parate'd.

They took off like rats in the sewer — after dropping their
bundles. They were in damn good shape having trekked, probably
multiple times a week, up and down canyon walls through the
desert for miles. And now, they had dropped the extra weight.
Typically, one bundle weighed anywhere from 25-50 pounds — some
were heavier, some were lighter, but that was the game. They
smuggled, we jumped them, they dropped it — abandoned. Minimal
paperwork, trophy shot. Everyone slept well.

But maybe not the mules that just lost their load.

West International

The area directly up against the physical border in Nogales,
Arizona was lined on both sides of the border fence (landing mat
metal from military excess fashioned into a physical barrier
separating the US and Mexico) with homes just feet from the border.

And on the US side, there was a street called West International,
or West "I." West I was pretty dangerous; multiple shootings
occurred in that area, and drugs were thrown over the border fence
to be collected by mules on the north side and very quickly taken to
a waiting vehicle or house.

One morning, as the sun was just starting to come up after a
midnight shift, our camera operators called out "Bundles coming
over the fence on West I." I was working nearby, but not assigned to
that area. However, no one answered on the radio. I wondered if
anyone was going to respond and after several minutes where no
one did, I answered that I would take it.

This would not be a case where the smugglers followed the rules.

As I was driving west on West I, a car sped down a driveway, and nearly T-boned me before the driver slammed on his breaks. I looked out my passenger side window and as I made eye contact with the two men in the car, I thought, "Huh, that's weird, they look super shocked to see me."

As mentioned in a prior chapter—I was a trained observer. It was maybe 6 a.m., and two young men hauling ass out of that neighborhood was a little suspicious. So, I put my truck in park, directly in front of their car, blocking them from proceeding and walked around the back of my truck to speak to the driver. As I approached the driver's side door, both he and the passenger got out of the vehicle.

Shit.

I asked them what they were doing down there and they answered with some nonsense. I then asked the driver if he would open the trunk so I could look inside.

I was still a very new agent, maybe on my own for a few months. Up until that point, I almost always had a Journeyman with me. Still, I referred to my training and started taking stock of my surroundings: the passenger of the car was trying to walk away or around me, or something, but it made me very uncomfortable as the driver handed me the keys to open the trunk.

I said, "No, you open it."

All I could think about was the horrible videos they showed us during the academy where an officer was overtaken and shot by subjects during a traffic stop. As the trunk popped open, I saw several bundles of what I suspected were drugs. Bundles are almost always wrapped on burlap sacks. These were those alright. Hundreds of pounds, easily.

I radioed over the net that I had 10-46 (code for drugs). Once you say that over the radio, everyone responds.

I noticed the passenger out of the corner of my eye, trying to almost tip-toe away. I drew my weapon and told him to come over to me, and for both of them to sit the eff down. I didn't know if he was trying to sneak up behind me or sneak away, but whatever he was planning, was not going to happen.

The driver did as told and sat down in front of me. The passenger started to walk toward me, but then abruptly turned away.

About that time, I heard and saw a beautiful white Bronco with the green stripe—one of ours—bounding down the border road in my direction, ass over elbows in a cloud of dust. If a truck could do that this truck was doing it. Holy shit, thank God, backup.

Mike M. —who was one of those agents you wanted in a shit situation—jumped out of his truck and I immediately told him, "That guy over there has been trying to get away." Mike, who was probably 6 foot, fit, and slim, took off after the passenger, who was only a small man, and apprehended him with little effort. He hadn't stood a chance.

I think the adrenaline dump hit me at that moment because I don't remember anything else until we unloaded the drugs back at the station. Trophy shot time. Another polaroid—this one of me carrying one of the bundles into the evidence room, with a big cheesy grin on my face—which is now tucked away in my little album. Ah, good times.

Escalada Drive Thru

As time went on, I became a Journeyman agent, and trainees were often assigned to me. On one such occasion, my trainee partner and I were assigned to an area known as the Escalada Drive Thru.

I had no idea why some of the landmarks were named what they were named, but this one was pretty obvious. It was the end of Escalada Street—which met the international boundary perpendicularly, and at some point in the past, cars could just drive through from Mexico. Illegally—this was not a port of entry.

At this point in time, however, there was that landing mat border fencing providing a barrier and preventing any vehicles from being able to drive across the border illegally. It was common for drugs to be thrown over the fence in this area, similar to West I. It was harder to see via camera, due to the lack of lighting and too many trees.

My trainee and I were working swing shift—always an activity-filled shift, especially after the sun set. Earlier in the shift, before the sun went down, the camera operators reported some activity on the south side of the fence. I was seasoned enough at this time to know this probably meant there would be activity later on. As the sun set, my partner and I hid our truck and walked up Escalada Street, attempting to conceal ourselves as we made our way up toward the border. There happened to be a car parked just north of the border fence in front of a house. There really wasn't anywhere else we could hide so we decided to lay in under the front of this car.

We waited a little while, not too long, before we heard rustling south of us as something or someone came over the fence.

Two thuds and running. Then, the trunk of the car we were laying under popped open and something dropped inside.

Shit—this was the load car.

As an individual was attempting to open the driver side door, my partner and I were scrambling like cockroaches to get out from underneath the front of it. The subject, shocked at us popping up from under the car, turned and attempted to run back to the border fence. We were able to catch him, get one small unimpressive bundle and call it a shift. Another polaroid for the album. Silly antics.

Chapter 8
Pivotal Moments

All things considered; those early years were a lot of fun. Learning the job, getting to know my coworkers, striking out on my own, and meeting the man who would become my husband. I was content, independent, and becoming more confident. My mom had come to live with me after losing her house and she was following a lifelong dream of hers — to work in the medical field. She was going back to school and becoming independent again. Arizona was good for us both.

All my classmates who were assigned to Nogales had made it through training and probation to be permanent agents. A lot happened in those first two years. Things that would determine my future, my decisions, my actions, and the choices I would make for the rest of my career and life.

In the summer of 1998, the thing you never truly believe will happen to someone you know, happened.

I was dating Ryan, my future husband, and working day shift. Ryan was on midnight shift at the time, a scope operator. He was also an agent, however, several agents on each shift trained to run the LORIS scope, another Vietnam-era type of technology that gave agents eyes in the dark via a camera or scope with infrared capabilities.

It was the morning of June 3, 1998, and as I pulled through the gate to the station, things just seemed off.

There were a lot more vehicles in the parking lot and around the station than there should have been, and people were milling about outside of the station. I found parking and proceeded toward the ramp up to the patio area just outside the doors of the station to report to muster at 7 a.m.

Ryan met me at the bottom of the ramp. This was odd. I mean, he often left a note or something in my car at the end of his shift, but I rarely saw him before muster. I was happy to see him. I asked him what was going on. He then broke the worst news possible;

An agent had been shot and killed that morning.

One of my classmates, Alexander Kirpnick.

My heart sank, complete and utter devastation in my soul.

You know as a law enforcement officer that these things can and do happen. You prepare yourself to face a situation in which you may be attacked or shot at—we train for that. We don't train for hearing the news that someone we know and care about was killed. No one does.

Alex and his partner had intercepted a group of drug mules. Once Alex had the mules on the ground, kneeling in front of him, one of them abruptly turned around and fired a shot that would take Alex's life. He was shot in the head. His partner called for help, giving the officer down code, and everyone and their brother responded.

Because the location was in the middle of a canyon, with only 4x4 access, the ambulance had to be escorted to the scene. My husband escorted the ambulance. He was on scene and witnessed the entire thing. I can only imagine the chaos and anxiety.

I went to muster after having a moment in the women's locker room.

This time I did cry.

One of the guys that I carpooled with — but for some reason hadn't carpooled that day — asked me what was going on and if I was ok. I told him that Alex had been shot and killed the night before. He was stunned. The leadership from the station called muster to order and we were addressed by a clinical psychologist. I have no idea what he said, I don't remember.

This would be the first and, unfortunately, not the last loss the agency would experience, or that I would experience in my career.

My supervisors did not assign me to the field that day.

One of my classmates was on shift with Alex when the shooting happened, helped the EMTs get him into the ambulance, and was never the same after that. He won't talk about it to this day.

I spent the morning calling my remaining classmates assigned to Nogales — we were spread out on different units by this time. I was the only one on the day shift, while 3 were on midnights (one now deceased) and the other 2 were on the swing shift. These were the worst phone calls I'd ever had to make in my life up to that point.

But I didn't want them to hear it from anyone else or turn on the news and see the story. I was the one to take responsibility, to get the job done.

None of us would be the same after that day.

Every agent on duty that night will forever have that radio traffic burned into the DNA of their memory. Every agent felt the loss of a brother or sister killed in the line of duty — even if you didn't have a personal relationship with them, even if you were not part of the same agency.

It's so hard to explain. The pain of that loss is so deeply seeded. I cannot adequately articulate the sorrow, sadness, lack of understanding, the asking "why" over and over again. We grieve for the loss and the senselessness of the death. They broke the rules of the game. They could have just taken off running. That was how it was done. The stakes just got really high.

His family suffered the worst loss, of course. The eldest child, the only son. His mother, his father, and his younger sister were all devastated.

Everyone knew who Alex was at the station. But for me, Alex was my friend. Alex would give the shirt off his back to just about anyone. Alex had been to my home.

Because we were all junior agents, we worked the holidays, so my mom would prepare a big old traditional meal for us for whichever holiday it was. I always invited the single agents without families in the area so they could have a good family meal and a sense of camaraderie on a holiday when they would have to report to work instead of spending time with their families, wherever they may be. Alex always came and he was the comedic relief. He had lived a life that most of us could only see in a movie.

He and his family were apparently once in the circus. They immigrated to the United States, escaping the harsh life in Soviet-era Ukraine. Alex spoke multiple languages — something like 5 or 6. Before his murder, he was called upon often to provide translation for Bulgarians, in particular. We had apprehended many groups with Bulgarians over the prior several months and instead of relying on translation services, the station relied on Alex.

Alex was a Ukrainian immigrant. After immigration to the United States, they settled in the Los Angeles area. He was very close to his sister. Alex had what could be described as a Russian accent. One of our Field Training Officers dubbed him "the Kirpinator," — an ode to the well-known Terminator movie star. Alex was the guy at the academy who offered to help me and my two female classmates with the Confidence course (otherwise known as the obstacle course, or the "C" course, for short), gave us tips, and so on.

Alex was the one who put himself out there, recognized we could use a little extra help, and offered, without expectation of a turnabout. He spent his off-time helping us and others in whatever way he could. While most of our classmates, us included, were out on a Saturday night relieving stress (i.e. drinking and dancing), Alex was not. And the next day when we were hung over, Alex offered to take us out to the "C" course for some extra training—as we had agreed upon before going out the night before.

Wait, maybe he was trying to teach us a lesson…

Kidding. He was a genuinely nice person.

Alex's funeral was held rather quickly in the Los Angeles area, as his family were of the Orthodox Jewish faith, which requires a fairly quick internment, so I was unable to go. However, the agency held a memorial sometime later, pulling out all the dogs and ponies. The United States Attorney, the highest-ranking official of the Department of Justice (DOJ) at the time, Janet Reno attended, as well as my entire class.

[This was pre-9/11, pre-Department of Homeland Security, so the US Border Patrol was part of the Immigration and Naturalization Service, which was part of the Department of Justice].

The ceremony was held at the Tucson Ball Park — I think it was called Electric Park at the time. Our classmates sat side by side in the first several rows of seats. Together again, but for the worst of circumstances. I remember the flyover, the rider-less horse walking across the field, taps being played, the 21-gun salute, each booming series going through me like thunder and the bagpipes — they get me every time.

It was ok to cry at a funeral or a memorial. And if you can hear Amazing Grace played on the bagpipes and not shed a tear, you are a better woman than I am.

One of the agents participating in the 21-gun salute gave me one of the shells at the end of the ceremony. I was honored to take it.

I try to go to funerals — to show my respect, to honor the life of the individual, and to show those remaining that they are supported. I was told once by a leader that her philosophy was, "Weddings maybe, funerals always."

Personally, I don't believe the funeral is necessarily for the person who died, but more for those left behind; so that we can have closure, say goodbye, have that release of emotion, and move on. Whenever someone says they don't want a funeral, all I can think is — it's not about you. It's about the people left behind.

It took a couple years for Alex's murderer to be identified, arrested, extradited from Mexico, and indicted. I don't remember his name. It's not important for this story. It's hard for my brain to comprehend, for a country with so much violence and cartel killings, that Mexico does not have the death penalty. So, for the United States to extradite anyone from Mexico, the US must agree that they will not seek the death penalty in a murder case.

In those two years, I had gotten married, lost my first baby, bought our first house, lost my best friend, Heather, and was pregnant again with my daughter by the time the trial started.

I asked my chain of command if I could attend, and they agreed. After a few days of testimony, the US Attorney's office contacted my station and requested that I be present for the remainder of the trial. Apparently, they felt that the jury was in some way connected to my presence. I wanted to be there anyway. I didn't know if they thought I was Alex's girlfriend or sister, but if they thought it would do any good, I would be there.

I sat through the testimony, listening to the replay of the radio traffic that night, dispatchers desperately listening for Alex to answer up on the radio, calling his star number several times to only silence. The testimony of the murderer's cellmate—describing how the subject told him the details of how he shot Alex that night. How he reached across his body and aimed the gun up, behind him, hitting Alex in the head. The forensics experts both described and showed how that story linked up to the trajectory of the bullet and the wound through Alex's brain.

I listened to the defense, disgusted by their attempts to make light of the situation. I specifically remember the defense attorney, a woman, questioning the lead FBI agent in the case. She opened by asking him his title to which he answered, "Special Agent so and so."

She then asked, "Special Agent? What makes you special?"

I think I audibly rolled my eyes in disgust. Who does that?

It was November of 2000, and I was very pregnant at the time. I went into labor, although I didn't know it was labor until later that evening, during the last days of the trial, sitting in the courtroom. I would not be present for the verdict, but the shooter was rightly convicted!

Several more months later, after my daughter was born and I was on maternity leave, I was notified when the sentencing would take place. You bet your ass I wanted to be there. The murderer was sentenced to life in prison. Worked for me. He deserved nothing less.

The Border Patrol is good at many things, and honoring our fallen is certainly top of the list. Alex's life and legacy will never be forgotten, and several people have made sure of that.

An agent's son, working toward his Eagle Scout certification, built a memorial at the site where Alex was shot. A large square stone foundation with a plaque inset on the top of it, describing what happened and when, and a pole rising out of the stone, affixed with the Star of David and just below, Alex's star number, N383. Forever retired from use, laid to rest with Alex.

Each new training class assigned to Nogales takes a trip out to the monument and they learn about what happened that night. A lesson about honor and remembering the fallen.

There is a plaque on the outside wall of the Nogales station, dedicating the building in Alex's honor. As you walk into the front visitor's entrance to the station, there stands a podium upon which is Alex's photo, news articles of his murder, and many other artifacts, including his credentials, up on the walls.

20 years after his death, I worked with Tucson Sector and Nogales station to hold a memorial in remembrance of Alex and his

sacrifice. The US Attorneys who worked on the case and prosecuted the murderer were in attendance, as well as Alex's sister and a childhood friend. Many of my classmates, most of whom had moved on or retired were present. And a large number of representatives from throughout the sector and other Agents who had since retired, returned for the occasion. News media covered the event, held at the location where Alex was shot, in front of his monument.

I can't thank the leadership of the sector at that time, Acting Chief Jeff Self, enough for their support and dedication to keeping Alex's memory alive. Jeff was once an agent in Nogales as well and was present on duty the night Alex was killed.

I don't think he would have been anywhere else that day.

It was important to honor Alex. And I was afforded the opportunity to speak at this event. My comments were simple — *Alex's death had such a huge impact because his life had a huge impact.* His sister and his childhood friend spoke as well, telling stories and honoring Alex's memory — with a similar theme — Alex taking care of others and offering help where he could, ever the optimist and comedian.

2023 marked the 25th year since Alex's murder. I again had the honor of attending and speaking during the dedication of the Nogales station gym in Alex's name. Fewer classmates could make it this time, but the station was very accommodating and obliged us with the honor of unveiling the plaque. Additionally, instructors for the station CrossFit program developed and named a workout after Alex — something that has been done for many fallen agents and soldiers. It is displayed with the other major workouts honorably named after the fallen, lining the walls of the gym.

One thing I really wanted to accomplish before I retired was to have the Nogales Station officially named after Alex, by Congressional proclamation. Unfortunately, current leadership in the Tucson Sector is not supportive, so it hasn't happened, yet. I'm not giving up as there are other avenues.

Daughter's Birth and LWOP

In early November of 2000, while attending the trial of my classmate's murderer, I started to feel like my back was hurting. I had back issues for many years, so it wasn't terribly alarming. I was about 37 weeks pregnant and had been sitting long days on hard courtroom benches. I was scheduled to be induced the following week.

Much like my first pregnancy, which I didn't catch at first either, I was having back labor. I didn't realize it until later on that evening after I had gotten home. My mom lived with us, so I told her I thought I was in labor, recognizing that the pain wasn't constant, but coming in waves. It was late and I knew it could take a long time so I decided to go to bed. I do love my sleep.

My husband was at work, on the afternoon shift at the time, working 3p-11p. I was jolted awake a few hours later by a real contraction, and waddled my way down the hall to my mom's room to tell her, I immediately had another contraction and called my husband to let him know. And then again after I got dressed because he was taking forever.

He had 3 kids already and thought the same thing I did — this could take a while, but the contractions were coming in quick succession. Only 3 minutes apart as we left for the hospital.

As soon as we got up to the room where I would deliver my daughter, and I had changed into the ever-lovely hospital gown, my water broke as I stood by a counter...

"EWWWWW," I said aloud.

"Oh, it's ok," the nurse said, "It happens all the time."

I was like, not to *me*.

Labor took all night. My daughter was born the next day, shortly after noon. She was sunny side up and had a cone head. She was a little over two weeks early from my due date, but come to find out, she would never be the one to be told when or what to do.

She was coming on her time, not mine.

I had asked for and was approved for a year leave without pay (LWOP). We had settled out of court for our previous baby's death. I had contracted a bacterium, called Listeria, from deli meat while I was pregnant with him which caused me to become very ill, and killed him in vitro. He was stillborn in late November, 1998. I was 26 weeks pregnant. We entered into a class action lawsuit against the company responsible and that money allowed me to be able to spend my daughter's first year of life watching and experiencing all of her firsts.

We named our son, Alex, after my classmate, who was killed only 5 months before I lost the baby. My daughter's middle name is Alexandra, after her brother and, of course, my classmate. It was an amazing year to be able to be present for everything a new baby experiences in their first year and I will forever be thankful for the person who mistakenly approved that request.

Yep… it wasn't supposed to happen. It never had before, and never has since. I was very fortunate.

Chapter 9
9/11 - The Day the World Stopped Turning

There is not a human of my generation or older who does not remember exactly what they were doing when they heard about the terrorist attacks of 9/11. Much like those who lived through any of the world wars, Pearl Harbor or any other major worldwide catastrophic event, it is burned into your memory forever.

I was home on maternity leave the morning of September 11th, 2001. My daughter was just 10 months old. I had finished feeding her when the phone rang. It was early in AZ, maybe 8 am.

On the other end of the phone was my mom, calling me from work, which she never did, very exasperated and telling me, "We're being attacked."

Now, she had a bit of a flare for the dramatic, so in my most practical tone, I asked her, "What are you talking about?"

She said, "Turn on the news. We are being attacked."

To this day, I don't watch the news of my own volition. If it's on, I'll watch, but I rarely turn it on. It's depressing. But, sure enough, I turned on the news and was glued to the TV for the next several days. I saw the second plane hit, and the live coverage of the towers crumbling to the ground. I could not believe what I was seeing and I could not wrap my head around the reality of it, the enormity of it. I thought, 'Well, I'm going back to work before my year is up.'

I didn't have to, thankfully, but when I did return in November, the border had changed. The world had changed.

My daughter doesn't know a time before 9/11. Now, there are several generations who never knew the world before 9/11. This was a pivotal moment in my career; in my life.

This and the death of my classmate may have affected my choices the most for the remainder of my career. They certainly altered the lens through which I viewed the world. A little less naïve, more real, cynical. Bad people existed and they did not care about anything beyond their own agenda and what it would take to accomplish it.

Chapter 10
I Don't Work for That Guy and Other Leadership Lessons

As my class neared the end of the academy, some of our instructors (all of whom were also agents — that's how the BP does it) gave us advice for when we hit the field. My Spanish instructor, a female agent, who would eventually transfer to Nogales as a supervisor, told us the following, "You'll have a good journeyman, and you'll have a bad journeyman, but you can learn from both."

I never forgot that, because it was so damn true. That same principle, I came to learn also applied to leadership, bosses, supervisors, and co-workers.

Back then, there wasn't any type of certification or course that a journeyman went through to qualify to teach trainees. If you had been in a year, you were considered a journeyman. Years later, the agency would formalize the field training units and field training officer training, as well as implement processes and procedures that every station must follow.

Not every journeyman is a training officer. They now must be certified as such. Evolution and progress.

Journeyman.

Doritos, the breakfast of Champions.

I was assigned to the dayshift, and I was eager to learn. I wanted to get out into the field, get my feet dirty, and become the best agent I could be. The dayshift wasn't typically very busy, so it was a time to get out into the field and learn the trails, interception points, and the overall area in the daylight.

I had been assigned to some great journeymen so far. I had a taste for what it was like. This pay period, though, I would be assigned to a very senior journeyman. He was a pro at processing, the paperwork side of the house. He'd probably been a BP agent for over 10-15 years at that time.

He was, however, not the type of guy I expected to be hiking the canyons with. He was not just overweight, but obese, and very unhealthy. The first thing we did after muster was drive to Burger King, where he ordered two meals and a large diet Coke — oh, the irony. We then proceeded to Circle K where he bought two full-size bags of Doritos. This would be our daily morning routine.

As we took our position overlooking the canyon we were assigned to, he dug his meaty, sausage fingers into one of the Doritos bags and then, to my great disgust, offered me some. No, thanks. This guy was also known for blatantly picking his nose.

Hard pass, not hungry.

I was assigned to ride with him for two weeks, a full pay period and the standard rating period for a journeyman and trainee. After those two weeks were over, I was looking forward to being assigned to a different journeyman.

I would be disappointed.

The scheduling supervisor assigned me to him for another two weeks.

He wasn't a bad journeyman from the perspective that he was not mean, and he didn't treat me badly. We drove around and he knew the area well. Until he needed a nap. This guy would fall asleep at his computer when processing a subject, wake up a few minutes later, and continue what he was doing. He still needed those naps out in the field.

I don't know if he had narcolepsy or if he had diabetes, or what — but, likely the latter.

He would park the truck, eat his greasy carb-filled breakfast, drink his diet coke — maybe that was supposed to negate everything else — and take a nap. He never missed a radio call though — that would wake him up. The ability he had to come to immediately was truly amazing.

Most days we were assigned the same position, Efraim Canyon. A busy canyon on any other shift, but closer to town and just a hop, skip, and a jump from West I. Just over the highway from the border. This was where they assigned him every single day — or in processing, but we weren't catching anyone, so we were out in the field.

I already knew I would not be this type of journeyman when my time came. I think the supervisors saw him as a liability, so they kept him assigned in close.

At the end of that second two weeks, I was frustrated.

I went to a supervisor, Mr. N, who had transferred to Nogales, and who coincidentally was an instructor for my class at the academy. He told me at one point before graduation when he knew he was also coming to Nogales, and that if I needed anything, let him know. Okey doke, I'm going to take you up on that offer.

He wasn't the scheduling supervisor but had access to the daily schedule. The scheduling supervisor was the only female supervisor on my shift. She was one of those females who was hard, or hardened. She did not take kindly to other women, or maybe just me.

I don't know what the issue was, but she was giving me crap assignments. I told Mr. N that I wasn't learning anything and wanted to know if I could get assigned a better journeyman. He took a look at the schedule and not only had I been with this same guy for a *month*, but I was about to be assigned another less-than-a-stellar journeyman for the next two weeks. He did me a solid and changed the assignment.

Later, that same female supervisor would be the one supervisor who always challenged me. She would call me out if my boots weren't shined, or if I left even a minute before 10 hours (we worked 10-hour shifts). And when I lost my first child, this supervisor, of all supervisors, would be the one who came to tell me that I wasn't allowed to go out to the field without a doctor's note clearing me. I would be assigned inside, with "light duty assignments" until such note was received.

Mind you, I never had a doctor's note saying why I was out for just two weeks after my baby died; just word of mouth.

I was devastated. I just wanted to get back to work.

I guess it was possible that the men didn't want to be the ones to do it, so they tagged her in. I think it was less the news she delivered and more the cold, bitchy way she delivered it. She didn't ask how I was; did I need anything — zero compassion. She told me I couldn't go out in the field and walked away. After I provided the doctor's note, she assigned me to downtown for a month straight.

When I became a supervisor, I eagerly volunteered to be the scheduling supervisor. I tried to rotate everyone, senior and junior agents, through the good assignments and the not-so-good assignments. I didn't play favorites. I didn't have favorites. I was as fair as I possibly could be without the union jumping down my throat.

Senior agents felt entitled to just about everything because they had tenure, the good assignments, the days off they wanted, the details, you name it. Not all of them, but the union was all about seniority. People could probably say a lot of things about me, but they couldn't say that I wasn't fair.

Don't speak unless spoken to

When I first started, we rotated shifts every four weeks. So in the year to come, as a trainee, I would be exposed to every shift at some point.

There were certain expectations of trainees. They get the truck ready, do all the pre-checks, gas it up, and so on. There were always some journeymen who thought they could treat trainees like dog poop or just plain, old, be an asshole. Some agents felt that because this was the way I was treated, you get shit treatment too.

Don't get me wrong, I had thick skin, I understood the razzing and NUG (New Guy) mentality toward trainees, but sometimes it went beyond that to a place that just isn't necessary. No one learns anything in that environment.

There were circumstances wherein journeymen dropped their trainees off on foot at the beginning of their shift, told them to hike out a trail, and picked them up at the end of their shift. I never had a journeyman treat me like that, but on one swing shift, my journeyman—who only had about two years in the service (he was my husband's classmate, I would learn later) —advised me when I got in the truck that I was not to speak unless spoken to and to stay in the truck unless he told me to get out.

My assigned journeyman, who would complete my evaluation for that pay period, was on days off. When that happened, trainees were put with just about anyone with a pulse. We were not allowed to work alone until after probation—this was a liability concern for the agency, so, I guess this guy was all they could offer that shift.

This shift will be a complete waste. Whatever, dude.

We were assigned to the far east and came upon another agent, Jaime (Do your best Spanish pronunciation because it's not JAY-MEE), who was cutting signs across a dirt road.

Cutting sign, simply stated, is following footprints and other disturbances to the environment that indicate humans or animals or whatever you're tracking, had trekked through the area. It is a skill that was adapted from native Americans and hunters over time, and most Border Patrol Agents worth anything are pretty adept at it.

We stopped and my journeyman got out of the truck, had a quick chat with Jaime, and proceeded to walk up the road a bit, mimicking what I had seen Jaime doing—looking at the ground.

Jaime came around to my side of the vehicle and asked why I hadn't gotten out. I told him that John told me to stay in the truck and not talk to anyone. Jaime muttered under his breath exactly what I thought— "asshole."

See, John was not known as a hard charger—he was balding, overweight, heading toward obese, with a large beer belly. He was a slug. He had no business trying to act like he was the big man on campus to a trainee. Jaime called him out on his nonsense. John sheepishly apologized and motioned for me to come and join them, loosening the reigns. But I was sure as hell not going to say anything to this guy or ask him any questions. Just needed to get through the shift.

In a stroke of luck, or maybe he was just trying to show off, we got on a group that another, very good sign cutter was tracking. We ended up going hill over dale—at a pretty fast clip, chasing this group most of the shift.

John brought up the back as I did my best to keep up with the guy I was chasing. The agent leading the charge called back to John at one point, giving him shit about being slow and out of shape. It turned out to be a worthwhile night, after all.

I realized something—this was one of those bad journeymen my instructor warned us about.

Lesson noted.

As valuable as anything else I could have learned that shift was this: This is NOT how you treat trainees. I always took the attitude that someday, this trainee could be my backup—and I would like them to respond with the fervor necessary to save my ass and know how to get to wherever I may be.

Bike Patrol

One of my favorite assignments as an agent was the timeframe I was on the bike patrol unit. I was in a unit with about 5 or 6 other agents, and the only female. This was in early 1999. We worked in the downtown area, with smaller, close to town canyons and the tunnels that ran underneath the whole of the city—both legitimate and illegitimate.

We were a tight-knit group and we mostly got along well. There was one guy on the unit that was a little strange—no one really wanted to be partnered up with him. I don't think he really wanted to hang out with most of us, anyway. The rest of us hung out on weekends, and had cookouts. Our husbands (well, mine) and wives got to know each other. We just clicked and had a lot of fun together. It made the shifts go really fast and some of the best times for sure.

On my first day on the bike unit, I was partnered up with Chris. I don't know how long he had been on the unit, but as a rite of passage, agents would ride down a particular set of stairs to "prove their awesome bike capabilities," I guess. Boys are weird. Anyway, Chris took me over to the set of stairs—a rather sketchy-looking set of stairs, concrete, with no railing. Before proceeding down the stairs with no issue, Chris said, "You don't have to do it."

UH – yeah, I do. I had ridden bikes all my life, I could surely handle this. Girls can do anything boys can do.

I was always a tomboy, to the extent that when I was 5, I thought I could run around with my brother and his friends with my shirt off—my mother did not agree. I always wanted to play football, but my mother did not agree.

About halfway down the stairs, I lost my nerve and my balance and tumbled the remaining way down, going over the handlebars and landed like a lump at the bottom. I scraped up my knee and my leg, but I was ok. The only thing that was truly hurt was my stupid pride.

I would not feel the need to prove myself again when challenged by a boy. Stupid games earn you stupid prizes.

The tunnels running underneath the city of Nogales ran south to north, and were built as drainage tunnels that originated from Mexico. The main tunnel was more of a riverbed—a concrete passageway through which you could drive a truck. In fact, when it rained, the water flooded this tunnel, the purpose for which it was built, and we would see all sorts of things floating in the water—everything including a yellow Volkswagen Beetle and dead bodies. True story. You did not want to be down there when it rained, even if it only rained in Mexico. It turned into a raging river.

Mexico, along this part of the border, sits higher in elevation than the US—thus, a need for water to pass, without impediment, or it would severely flood Mexico and downtown Nogales, AZ.

The underground tunnels were great for smuggling, both people and narcotics. They mostly used the legitimate tunnels and popped up at certain manholes or drainage points, got topside, and took off toward the taxi lots or a waiting load-car. The smugglers used car jacks to jack up the manhole covers and grates to pass their product through, be it human or narcotic.

My bike unit partners and I would typically set up, out of sight, to watch the manholes and drainage points where we knew someone or something was likely to pop up. Once they did, all we had to do was get on our mountain bikes, ride over, and make the arrests.

There was one drainage grate in particular that the smugglers kept jacking open. It didn't matter what we did, or what giant boulder we put on top of it, it never held them off.

We had a welding crew that would go around on dayshift, and weld shut the broken open grates and manholes. It was a major safety issue for people to pop up in the middle of a street out of a manhole, first of all, for them and anyone driving down that street. But the smugglers had massive hydraulic jacks and popped the welds anyway like they were nothing.

One morning, we showed up to get in our hiding spot and noticed an engine block atop one of the grates. An. Engine. Block. Where the hell?

Apparently, as we found out later, in the dark of night, agents located, secured, and dragged an engine block behind one of the trucks, sparks flying everywhere, grating along the road, digging ruts in the pavement, to place upon the grate so that the smugglers couldn't get it open.

I think their true purpose in putting the engine block over the grate, was so that they didn't have to sit and watch it.

Bike patrol agents didn't work on midnights, so an agent would have to sit an X at those points without something like an engine block. Agents can be very creative and crafty when properly motivated. It was much more satisfying to work the far-out canyons than to sit on an X in the middle of town.

The engine block worked for a while, but then one day, it was gone. Probably removed by the smuggler's associates on the US side of the border.

Oftentimes, smugglers dug illegitimate tunnels off the legitimate tunnels, most of which ended up dug up through the floor of a stash or load house. Some of the tunnels were dug from a warehouse or house in Mexico, under the border, and came out in a house or warehouse in the US. It was very difficult to detect such activity.

The ingenuity of the smugglers always amazed me—if only they used their powers for good! Some of these tunnels were high quality, dug with the precision and safety of tunnels/shafts dug for mining. Maybe they hired miners, or engineers, who knows? Smuggling probably paid better than mining, with tunnels reinforced by 2x4s and fresh air being pumped in via hoses.

However, some of the cruder tunnels caved in and one day agents would come across a hole in the ground that shouldn't have been there, and voila—a tunnel was discovered. Nogales and San Diego were famous for the tunnels. They still find tunnels today.

I always thought that someday the whole city of Nogales would collapse with all the illegitimate tunneling that went on. It hasn't yet.

At the end of our shift, oftentimes, we would go down in the tunnels to clear them out, so the next shift had time to get out into the field and take their positions. We would drop down in the large culvert and walked south towards Mexico.

We wore our night vision goggles, or at least one person would wear the only pair we had, and the rest of us would line up behind them and walk with one hand on the shoulder of the person in front of us, like a tactical team making an entry into a building. But our tactics were so we all stayed together—because only one person could see.

If we came across anyone, and we usually did—we'd turn on our flashlights and arrest them. Or they would run south and cross back into Mexico. The boundary between the US and Mexico underground was marked, though not very well.

Eventually, there was a gate installed that lifted whenever the flooding water flowed through. It was supposed to be too heavy for a person to push it open, but that good ole ingenuity again—they always figured out a way.

As you can imagine, like any place where humans sit or gather for long periods, the tunnels were full of trash, human excrement, and God only knows what else.

One of the guys on the unit, Jared, never once came out after clearing the tunnels without feces on him somewhere. Human feces. Poor bastard.

We would often have to get on each other's shoulders to climb out of the tunnel at times, depending on where we decided to exit. One particular day, we had done our walk south and had come back north as Jared proclaimed, "I finally made it without getting crap on me."

That day, Jared was the lucky one who had to lift one of the other guys on his shoulders, and upon doing so, smelled something. He looked down at his shirt, only to find the other agent had left him a lovely present from his shoe.

He did not ever, that I can remember, come out of the tunnels without human excrement of some kind somewhere on his person.

I don't want to work for that guy

I returned from maternity leave a few months after the terrorist attacks on 9/11. I was back on a unit, working the dayshift — I had a bit of seniority at this time, not hard to do when trainees were rolling in monthly. And instead of rotating shifts every 4 weeks, the station had gone to a bid for a shift system. Mostly based on seniority, so agents put in their request for a shift, days, swings, or mids; 1st and 2nd choice, sometimes a 3rd, depending on how junior one was. And in concert with the union, supervisors made the assignments to shifts. If an agent didn't get their first choice two rotations in a row (we did 6-month rotations), they were guaranteed it on the third rotation.

People generally liked this method — at least they could plan their lives a little better for 6 months at a time, instead of rotating every 4 weeks. Rotating shifts wreaked havoc on your mind, your body, and your family. We also shifted from rotating days off to requesting days off. This was mostly based on seniority as well. I always liked to have a weekday off, so I generally asked for Sunday and Monday.

A few months after returning from maternity leave, there was a supervisory announcement for those who wished to be promoted. Some of those receiving promotions were obvious choices, however, I could not believe my eyes when I read one of the names: John — the journeyman who told me to stay in the truck and not speak unless spoken to — was going to be a supervisor.

I thought, what the actual?

I mean, you take a test and get a score, and some people are just good test takers, but how in the hell could anyone think this guy should be in any type of supervisory role, with people reporting to him?

I knew at that moment that I would put in for the next round of promotions, because there was no way in hell, I wanted to work for someone like that. And that was it—the reason I decided to put in for my first promotion.

Things were good for me. I was on the shift I wanted to be on—convenient for a new mom. Getting the days off I wanted—convenient for relationship time with my husband and taking my mother-in-law to church. But I could not fathom or stomach the idea of working for someone who I absolutely did not respect.

I took the test, made the list, and as you already know, I was selected because they had to select a female (wink, wink). That was June of 2002. The Patrol Agent in Charge of the station called me at home on my days off, which really caught me off guard. Why was the big boss of the station calling me at home?

I remember very distinctly answering the phone while holding my daughter when he offered me the position. He asked me to report the next day I worked, wearing bars and ready to jump into the role. Yes, sir, you got it. I stayed on dayshift until it was official and then they put me on midnights—I just moved back to the bottom of the totem pole.

The theme of not wanting to work for certain people carried through the remainder of my career. Either that thought, or 'Heck, if that guy can do the job, I sure as hell can do it.'

I saw people getting promoted around me but I could not understand what leadership saw in them.

Leadership lessons that stick

Warren

I was a brand-new supervisor in September of 2002, assigned to the midnight shift for about 3 months. Every supervisor had a certain number of agents assigned to them for performance rating purposes. At that time, it was approximately a 1 to 7 ratio. I had to evaluate and provide a score for each of those 7 agents based on the established rating criteria.

One of the agents assigned to me was Warren. I hadn't worked with him in the past so I didn't know his work ethic, regular actions, whether or not he was a hard charger or slug but I did know that he didn't have a bad reputation. So I expected he was a decent agent.

Over time, I noticed that Warren was hard to find on shift.

He would pretty much disappear after muster. He didn't answer the radio and he didn't seem to be working traffic. I assumed, based on that, that he was a slug, lazy no-good agent who "worked" midnights for the extra money, but went off to hide and probably sleep all shift.

I decided I was going to ding him on his performance evaluation. When I approached my supervisor to get his ok, he told me, no, that I couldn't give him that rating. I was only going to rate him as unsatisfactory in one area and satisfactory overall—the general thought back then was anything less than above satisfactory was a failure and "we didn't do that." I wasn't happy about it, but I begrudgingly changed his rating and gave him his evaluation.

I found him somewhere deep in a canyon, where I assumed he had gone to take a nap, when I served him. So, I was especially annoyed.

Fast forward about 3 months, still working midnights, Christmas Eve, sometime during the swing shift because my husband was at work.

My husband notified me while he was on shift that an agent was in his home and threatening suicide. The agent had called his brother, who was out of state, who then called the station to get some help. My husband responded to the agent's house along with some other Border Patrol Agents and supervisors as well as local law enforcement. After many hours of attempting to get the agent to not hurt himself, he committed suicide.

It was Warren.

It hit me like a ton of bricks.

Because what I didn't do as his supervisor, and I will regret it until the day I leave this earth, was to get to know him. I didn't try to find out if this was a change in behavior for him. I didn't ask anyone. You can't help people if you don't know what is going on with them.

Warren was going through a divorce, depressed and alone on Christmas Eve and it was more than he could deal with. He was facing the prospect of losing his kids, at least from his perspective.

What if I had taken the time to talk to him about my observations of his performance, rather than taking the stance that he must be a bad agent? I didn't display a single ounce of leadership. It was a very hard and devastating lesson.

I may have overcorrected moving forward, but I made it a goal of mine to get to know anyone who worked for me. I told this story every single chance I got to new supervisors, because it was so important to me to impart to them the valuable lesson of taking care of *your people*.

Taking opportunities

Once I became a first-line supervisor, I thought, 'This is good, I could do this for the rest of my career.' Especially after we moved to Erie, PA and our neighborhood was perfect for raising a young child — 4 or 5 houses all with little girls the same age as my daughter. I thought they'd grow up together and be the best of friends. I would prove myself wrong.

After the second winter that extended into June, I remembered why I wanted to leave the Northeast in the first place. And headquarters was asking my husband why he wasn't putting in for jobs. Erie was a career dead end. My husband and I were the only two supervisors at a station with 6 agents — that included us, 3 frontline agents, and our boss, the Patrol Agent in Charge (i.e. commander of the station). We couldn't do that for another 10-15 years; we would both go insane.

I never had a rigid plan, and I didn't put a limit on the time I was going to be in any position. I have run across agents over the years who would say to their boss, "I'll give you 1 year and then it's time to move onward or upward."

A little arrogant, I always thought, considering there is a lot to learn in any level of supervision. Depending on where you work, one year may be 5 years' worth of learning the job or it may be 5 months' worth.

It was vastly different in Erie than in Nogales, I can attest to that.

I took the opportunities as they presented themselves. I certainly never thought I would end up as an executive. I was nervous just calling out roll call in the front of the muster room. I was not comfortable speaking in a public setting. My voice cracked and trembled, which just made me more insecure about it. I eventually got over that, at least for muster purposes.

As my career progressed and we moved around, usually when my husband got a promotion, the organization would get a two-for-one deal. Of course, they knew they wanted him, but I came as a bonus (cheesy smile).

There were comments now and then that I'd find out someone said, "She only got the job because she's riding her husband's coattails."

Whatever makes you feel better about yourself.

I never took a spousal transfer. I was able to attain a position wherever we went, competitively or via lateral transfer. I don't think I was ever promoted when we transferred somewhere—I either took a lateral or busted down and then worked my ass off to prove myself and would get promoted as time went on. On my own accord, without the support of my husband's coattails.

What is busting down, you ask? Let me give you a scenario.

I was a GS-14 Assistant Chief at Headquarters when my husband was offered a Patrol Agent in Charge (PAIC) position in South Texas—another scenario where a leader called him and asked him why his name wasn't on a list. He put in the next go-around and was selected. I would also need a job, but I fully realized that I should return to the field, either at the same or only one step above the position I left.

I put in a lateral reassignment request for a second level, GS-13 Field Operations Supervisor position, the next logical step above a first-line supervisor, at a station. I was selected, begrudgingly, by the PAIC of McAllen station. When he called me to offer me the position, he as much as told me that he was forced to pick me, and his tone of voice made it clear that he was not at all pleased with the prospect.

I offered to provide him with my resume, so he could call my references. I'd been a supervisor for 5 years before coming to DC, after all, and I was very excited at the opportunity. And I had just earned my master's degree.

"No thanks," he said, completely unimpressed.

Great, can't wait to get there.

There you have it, I busted down from a GS-14 to a GS-13, taking a step down on the ladder, if you will.

I enjoyed my time back on the line and in the field. I didn't mind being on different shifts, in fact, I looked forward to it. My husband was straight dayshift so that eased the burden and guilt with our daughter. I was also afforded the opportunity to work on a shift with someone I knew from Nogales — Charlie, who had transferred from there. I must admit, it was nice and made things a little smoother to have someone who already knew me at the station. He knew my work ethic and my reputation, but he also knew people from 'the valley,' as it's referred to. He had grown up there.

The Rio Grande Valley is a tough Sector to break into if you didn't start your career there. I don't know why, but they seemed to think that South Texas was the only place in the patrol where anyone could possibly become a good agent.

And, oh my god, I was "from" headquarters.

They hated headquarters and had no respect for anyone "from" headquarters as if we started our career there and never had any field time. That was the chip on a lot of people's shoulders, especially the PAIC who offered me the job. Granted, most of these folks at the station had never been to headquarters, so there was that.

The PAIC had people he wanted to promote from within, which is totally fair, but I had pushed in and taken that opportunity away from them. Not sorry. RGV rarely brought anyone in from another sector, particularly in a promotion scenario. It was made up of mostly originals.

A lot of agents had grown up in the valley, gotten back to their mecca, and would never leave. I had heard the valley referenced since the academy. Most people from there wanted to get back there. I only met one agent, in 27 years, that was from the valley and had no desire to go back there.

I get it – their entire families were there.

But I would be willing to give it a chance if they were willing to give me a chance.

Please refer to me, henceforth, as Master.

Let me just step back a bit, to while I was still assigned to HQ. It will help put into context future opportunities while assigned in South Texas.

I was serving as the adjutant to the Southwest Border Chief — the person in charge of all the Chiefs at the 9 sectors along the southern border. This was not my calling. I hated it. I was, more or less, responsible for making sure my principal had what he needed for meetings, would travel with him, make his travel plans, take notes, make sure he had food, work with his assistant on his calendar, and so on.

I am not what I would consider a person who likes to serve others in this capacity, and this was way too much of that. I took the opportunity because I was asked specifically by my principal, someone I'd known working in Nogales. It was a great opportunity to get to sit in high-level meetings and be exposed to the inner workings of the higher echelons of government.

But I needed to be challenged, so I was looking for something else.

I had never really thought about furthering my education beyond earning my bachelor's degree — until an opportunity presented itself.

An announcement came out that DHS offering a select few positions in the Naval Postgraduate School, Center for Homeland Defense and Security (NPS, CHDS) master's degree program. On their dime.

It was a new program that stood up in the wake of 9/11, offering higher education in all things related to Homeland Security. It was an 18-month program, composed of both virtual and on-site learning requiring a thesis at the end to graduate. The program was offered to state, local, and federal agencies — any that had any sort of role in Homeland Security, ranging from infrastructure protection to emergency management, to the US Coast Guard, to local police and fire departments, and so on. I had classmates from all of those disciplines, plus the FBI, TSA and more that I can no longer remember.

Some of the master's degree programs offered by the DOD war colleges were only 10 months long, but they required one to be away, attending classes every day as if they were off to college.

I didn't want to leave my family for that extended period, so I thought this program would be perfect if I could get in. My daughter was about 8 and my middle stepson, 15 at the time, had come to live with us. Several agents were going through the DOD schools, or had been through them, but at this point, no Border Patrol Agent had ever attended the Naval Postgraduate School program.

Cool, let me give this a whirl.

A few months later, I found out that I had been accepted into the program. No shit! A few months after I started with the master's program, I was then detailed to the Department of Homeland Security to work as a CBP liaison on their crisis response planning team—another opportunity that just kind of showed up at the right time. It was a great mix—as a detailer, I was serving in a different capacity at a new location, and I was never on call, only assigned to represent a sector, operationally. And I could focus on homework during my time off.

18 months later, after way too much reading, homework, presentations, papers, and a 60-ish page thesis, I graduated with my Master of Arts in Security Studies. One of the proudest moments of my adult life.

Please refer to me, henceforth as Master Scudder.

My mother wasn't sure I was smart enough for a four-year degree, and I wasn't the best student in high school. Unfortunately, she didn't live to see this accomplishment, but I know she would be proud.

People would ask, "Are you going for your PHD next?"

Oh, God, no, if I never read a book again that's not for pleasure, it will be too soon. One of our instructors told us at the beginning of the program, "It's only a lot of reading if you do it."

I did it. I can't sit down and enjoy a book to this day. That may not be 100% a product of this program — probably involves some other things, like high cortisol levels — but that's a topic for another chapter.

I made some amazing connections during the program. A large byproduct of that type of engagement was network building. Networking may have been the most important result, in fact. One of my classmates became the Acting Commissioner of CBP. Pretty impressive.

These two opportunities combined catapulted my career: getting my Master's degree and being detailed to the Department.

Opportunities to Go and Grow and Lot Lizards.

Not everyone appreciates the accomplishment of higher education.

In fact, in the Border Patrol, you are not required to have any type of degree to qualify for any position, even the highest position in the nation. While we were encouraged by the higher levels of leadership to apply for these programs, there was no promise that it could or would give anyone an advantage. In fact, it would be illegal to consider someone with a degree over anyone else — giving them points, for example, on a hiring matrix if the degree is not a requirement for qualification for the job.

So, why bother?

I answer that by simply saying: for the education itself. For the experience and the personal accomplishment. While it may not matter internally to the USBP, by and large, there may be instances or opportunities in the future when it does matter. Plus, my mom would be super proud of me.

Having said that, some leaders within the organization did pay attention to those who took on the challenge to accomplish this, and one, in particular, was the Deputy Chief of the Rio Grande Valley (RGV) Sector. He had the attitude that since the government paid for this education, the agency should damn well put it to use.

Put me in, coach.

I held four positions in four years while stationed in RGV. The first year, I was a FOS on a shift at the McAllen station. Word was getting around that I had my master's degree and had been part of department-level planning. Turned out that not everyone thought people from HQ were a waste of space. The Assistant PAIC of Intel had done a short tour at HQ, knew who I was from his time there, and inquired with my station command as to whether I could come up to Sector Intel for a few weeks and do an internal sort of audit of their programs—leverage some of those skills I learned during the master's program and my time at the department.

I think they were actually testing me out to see if they wanted to bring me up to work for them in Intel, but who knows? They were offering me an opportunity to do something different and stretch my academic muscles, so I was game. There was an announcement for a Special Operations Supervisor (SOS) position within Intel around that time. I went ahead and applied — you can't win if you don't play. It was equivalent to the position I held in the field, but Intel-focused, not strict line operations.

In the RGV, the Intel program was, at that time, the dumping ground for programs that they didn't know where else to put them. They had two programs that I couldn't figure out how they fit under Intel: Prosecutions and Planning. They could only reason that "they" didn't know what else to do with them.

Tactical operations planning is one thing. Longer-term contingency and campaign planning are very different. I had experience in all three.

DHS at this time was venturing into integrating its components — operationally — to more efficiently address tactical situations on the border. DHS planners, where I was previously detailed, put together an initiative at the request of the DHS Secretary, designed to integrate all of the maritime capabilities they possessed — US Coast Guard, CBP Immigration and Customs Enforcement, and Homeland Security Investigations (ICE, HSI), the investigative arm of DHS.

In theory, this effort would bring to bear all the assets DHS had available, combine them, and create Regional Coordinating Mechanisms (ReCoM) to address illegal maritime traffic throughout the nation. The command was a loose sort of unified command, with a core leader ordained by DHS.

I was tapped to lead the creation of the Corpus Christi ReCoM planning and implementation. The executive lead for the Corpus Christi ReCoM effort was the Admiral from the US Coast Guard district in which Corpus Christi sat.

What? Now I work for the Coast Guard?

The leaders from the respective agencies involved sat on a board — if you will, the unified command, and the Admiral managed it, kept people on task and in line, etc. My Chief was one of these leaders. I got paid by the Border Patrol, but I was now responsible to DHS.

I'm sorry, how did I get here?

I worked with peer-level representatives from each of the respective participating agencies and we accomplished what we set out to. We developed a plan to integrate our agencies to combat maritime crime. Thus, the Corpus Christi ReCoM was born.

Sometime during that effort, I was selected for that SOS position in Intel I had put in for. I wasn't sure if I wanted to accept the position though.

I had a conversation with my buddy, Charlie, telling him this: I was enjoying my time on the shift, back in the field.

He gave me this advice, "You would be stupid not to take this job. It's day shift and you will be closer to home."

Damn, common sense.

This was the second position I held in RGV. I was also dubbed the Chief of Staff (not a real position and not a pay raise) for the Corpus Christi ReCoM. It was an operational group, working day and night, in the maritime domain. They made arrests, we implemented operations, caught bad guys, drugs, and all the maritime border crime. We held monthly briefings for the Unified Command under the watchful eye of DHS — responsible for making this a worthy effort, which it was. But this was a lot of pressure from on high that this area had not experienced. I didn't mind the extra work; I liked to be busy.

I eventually received the Department of Homeland Security Secretary's Silver Medal for my efforts with this initiative.

A bit later, DHS came out with a plan to integrate the same agencies, led by CBP, along the land border — thus, the South Texas Campaign was born.

I didn't want to do it again, so I tried to stay away from the effort and remain unseen, doing my job as an SOS in Intel. I was also still the Chief of Staff for the ReCoM. I had a great team and was getting to do some pretty cool field stuff, Intel-related, but operational.

I was leading a team investigating, in concert with HSI, a transnational criminal organization (TCO) that was known to use semi-truck air dams to transport illegal aliens.

If you look at a semi-truck, some of them have an area above the cab that sits up high, almost like a spoiler, but the reverse. It serves to move air above and over the truck for efficiency's sake, I imagine. Anyway, there is an empty space on the backside in which several humans can fit and hide.

The Border Patrol checkpoint, located in Falfurrias, TX had intercepted several of these semis, with people stashed up inside the air dams. The drivers typically did not know they were transporting people up there.

It was an incredibly dangerous place to catch a ride, to say the least, for multiple reasons. After some observation, investigation, and research, my team determined that the smugglers were using a truck stop as the point where the aliens would either be dropped off or have to walk to and find a truck with an air dam. Once the driver was out of sight, the people would climb up in the air dam and settle in for a long ride.

I had an agent on the team who held a commercial driver's license and thus could drive a semi. Fortunately, RGV also recently seized a semi-truck and trailer.

Bingo. We had our stakeout situation figured out.

We drove the semi to the truck stop, parked it near the other semis, and waited. We'd placed cameras on the back of the semi's trailer, camouflaged so most normal passersby would not know what they were, but situated so that we could see the people, once dropped off, as they approached the truck stop from the road.

Something you should know about truck stops that I never knew before this operation.

There are women, known as "lot lizards," who sell their wares to truck drivers for a price. They go from truck to truck offering their services. Yes, prostitutes who focus their sales on truck stop parking lots. I had no clue this was a thing. Stand by for why that matters.

As our operation progressed, we were able to notify agents standing by to pull over the semi-trucks and retrieve the people hiding in the air dams shortly after they left the parking lot.

However, this didn't serve to provide us with the necessary information to proceed with the investigation and build a case. We needed to find out *where* they were taking them. We identified common vehicles and individuals in the area who would follow the trucks through the checkpoint and the next time they stopped, offload their cargo and carry on.

We decided to allow one semi — that we observed — be loaded and to drive through the checkpoint. But we wanted to make the driver aware of his cargo. So, in plain clothes, I approached this semi-truck, knocked on his passenger side door, jumped inside, and showed him my badge. I informed him of who I was, the agency I was with, and what was going on.

No one outside saw me show him my badge. I was in plain clothes, hair down, wearing a zipped hoodie. A few days later, we started to hear chatter via some of our informants, that there was a new lot lizard at this truck stop.

Wait, what?

"Some blonde, white chic," they informed us.

Those watching thought I was a 'lot lizard.' Dammit.

I didn't know how to feel about being mistaken for a prostitute. I guess that was better than blowing our cover.

I did not approach a semi driver again like that. I'm pretty sure that for a second or two, that driver had thought he was about to get propositioned.

Eventually, we had enough evidence to take down the TCO and that operation was put to bed — a pretty good success — and a lot of fun. It's always fun to put smugglers in jail.

Don't be a dick!

Alas, my prior success with the ReCoM was out.

The Chief of the RGV Sector called me into his office one day. I had applied and interviewed for several GS-14 positions throughout the Sector and was hoping this was going to be an offer for one of them. In fact, it was.

He offered me an Assistant Chief Patrol Agent position—regaining the GS-14 grade.

He said to me, "You have a reputation for building things, so we want you to take over the McAllen Area Team."

Although I did not previously want to be involved with it, the South Texas Campaign (STC) was in full swing, and the McAllen area team was part of it. I couldn't avoid it any longer.

The area of responsibility for the STC incorporated three sectors, Rio Grande Valley (RGV), Del Rio, and Laredo, TX—each of which had its own smaller command and operational groups, called area teams. A Commander, situated in Laredo—as he was the Laredo Sector Chief—now doubly tasked, had oversight for the operations that were part of this effort. He was given both tactical and administrative control of all the assets throughout the corridor.

Although I had done something similar, I felt wholly unprepared for this task. There would be many times to come when I felt this way.

RGV Sector was now the center of the border universe. Traffic in this area had increased to levels never experienced, the busiest in the nation. Agents were apprehending thousands of people of multiple nationalities and demographics daily. McAllen station was getting hit hard with human traffic, particularly unaccompanied juveniles, while stations to the west were seeing increased drug trafficking.

Any way you looked at it, we were understaffed and over-pressured to handle the influx. Gone were the days of just

Mexicans— we saw more than 100 different nationalities that year, primarily from Latin American countries. Logistically speaking, things just got a lot more challenging. Everyone along the immigration continuum had to come into the sandbox and was ready to play. The Border Patrol apprehension was only the first step in a long process.

I was thrust into the limelight, tapped to lead another effort related to the buzzword of the decade, integration.

My team included agents and officers from CBP's three operational components: USBP, Air and Marine (AMO), and the Office of Field Operations (OFO—the folks in blue uniforms who work at the Ports of Entry), as well as representatives and partners from the DEA, FBI, ICE, and the US Attorney's office. It was an all-out effort to curb, stop, and put an end to the craziness going on along the border.

The goals and targets were lofty — to arrest and prosecute those at the very top of the criminal organizations ultimately responsible for the activity along the border, some of whom never crossed the border into the US.

Integration, in theory, is a great idea. How could things possibly go badly if we all worked together?

In reality, it is incredibly difficult.

First, someone has to be in charge. No one and everyone wants to be in charge at the same time. What I mean by that is that people want their interests met, and they participate when it suits them. Being in charge carries with it the responsibility for success and the accountability for failure. Although I was the McAllen Area team lead, the Chief of the RGV Sector, my chief, was ultimately accountable for whether we succeeded or failed.

As I came into my role, the team had just suffered a major blow.

There were monthly briefings to the Commander, during which each area team would describe their progress, their operations to date, and so on. Word had gotten down to everyone that the McAllen area team's latest brief was awful. It wasn't what the Commander was expecting, or looking for. They had completely missed the target, and the Chief took the brunt of that ire. They were not in a good place.

I was about to step into my role and the guy who was currently over the team would be asked to step aside but stick around. Ouch.

I didn't know how to deal with that situation, and we had two weeks to get our collective crap together as we were expected to re-brief the Commander at that time.

During this same time, I was attending the CBP Leadership Institute — a CBP leadership training that was meant to prepare the next generation of agency leaders. It was an opportune time because that training offered me several tools, without which I could not have been successful.

This Chief almost always ended meetings by saying, "Failure is not an option."

And I would audibly roll my eyes. The fuck, it isn't.

Sometimes failure is the only option, pal, and the thousands of times we have all failed proves that. Didn't you, didn't *we*, just fail? Talk about pressure.

I had what I had as far as team composition. In government, and many jobs, I'm sure, when you enter a leadership position, the team is already in place. You didn't pick them, but now this is what you have, and you need to lead them to success, or failure (wink).

As mentioned earlier, we had two weeks to re-frame, re-plan, and re-do what did not please the Commander the first time. We gathered daily, bringing all the needed members of the team together. We needed information from Intel investigators, some of which weren't keen on sharing information in the past, and generally the operational posture along our section of responsibility. We wrote, we corrected, we developed presentations and charts depicting who was who in the criminal zoo, which agencies had warrants or investigations on them, and put all of this together for a pre-brief to the Chief. I guess, I'll give him a name now — Chief H. The Deputy was Deputy L.

The day and time of the pre-brief had arrived. It did not start well and it only went downhill from there.

My team could not prepare the room ahead of time and was having difficulty getting the computer to boot up when Chief H walked into the room. Granted, he was a minute or two early, but he was visibly displeased. He took his seat, huffed loudly, stood up, said, "Come and get me when you are ready," and walked out of the room.

I don't know about you, but I did not feel like that was a good sign. Great, like I wasn't already nervous.

I had not kicked the nerves associated with briefing people by this time — I never really would — so I was about to go throw up. My digestive system always paid for my nervousness. TMI, not sorry.

We got the audio/video system working and invited Chief H and Deputy L back into the room. They sat down, and Chief H, as he always did, leaned way back in his chair and put his big gouty, chubby foot on the table, showing off his ridiculous white tube socks sticking out above his black ankle boots.

Who wears white tube socks anymore — much less in uniform? And seriously dude, this isn't a spa.

To quickly describe the personality of Chief H, suffice it to say, he was like the high school football player, a bully type of guy. Not a starter, but good enough to get the letterman's jacket, who still thought he was God's gift to the Border Patrol. Arrogant, but not earned arrogance, from my perspective. Sometimes it was just who you knew.

In my opinion, he wasn't attractive, he wasn't kind, and he wasn't funny — so I'm not sure what fueled his arrogance. There is definitely a brotherhood in the valley that is hard to describe.

Anyway — I began to give the brief, one slide at a time when Chief H started barraging me with questions.

I said, "Chief, if you let me get through the brief, your questions will be answered."

That just pissed him off. I never got off the first slide. He said something to the Deputy, got up again, and stormed out of the room. Well, shit. I guess failure was an option here.

Deputy L stayed behind and attempted to give me some guidance. However, this is how he spoke: some words and then "Ya know, what I'm sayin'?" Some more words, and then "Ya know what I'm sayin'." These were not complete thoughts. I did not know what the hell he was saying. I wasn't about to admit that.

He drew a diagram on a piece of paper and off I went to figure this out. Thankfully, the PAIC of Intel was also in the room and he understood 'what he was sayin'.' More likely, he had insight because he often met with the Chief and the Commander.

We worked together to amend what my team had fixed once already and put together the brief to give to the Commander. We did not have time to re-pre-brief Chief H, as we had to be in Laredo in two days. He was only able to review the briefing deck. I'm sure he was stressed and nervous—his motto of 'failure is not an option' wasn't looking so good.

I felt like we had a good product and would be able to meet the expectations of the Commander. A few of my team and I traveled to Laredo and I practiced and practiced that brief. I wrote it out and narrowed it down to talking points on flashcards that I could reference if I got super nervous and couldn't remember anything. I practiced the night before, that morning, and on the drive to the briefing.

Oh, my tum-tum. Nothing I had eaten or drank for the last three days was left in my body. It had divested itself of everything. I was nauseous, dehydrated, and had a headache.

But I still had epic RBF, so no one was the wiser.

We stepped into the small conference room, with a small table set up in the middle of the room, but situated more toward the far end. The Commander and his staff shortly walked out of a door behind the table. There were chairs set up along the walls around the room as well, I guess for an audience. Oh, goody.

We were to sit on our side of the table. The table was maybe 2-3 feet across, not very wide. I could have reached across the table and touched the elbow of the man across from me — the Commander. I was not going to do that. I set down my notecards, handed out the presentations, and prepared to start, upon the Commander's go-ahead.

Chief H and Deputy L were video teleconferenced in on a small screen up on the wall to my right, the Commander's left. They clearly did not have 100% confidence in my ability to pull this off. Well, me neither buddy.

The Commander gave the go-ahead and I began. As soon as I spoke, my hands shook, but as I got into a groove, I didn't even need the note cards. Everything was flowing along nicely.

Until the Commander asked a question.

Before anyone in the room could answer, Chief H came over to the video teleconference, interrupted, and started to speak. I don't remember what the question was or what the answer was, but I clearly remember this:

The Commander stood up, as the Chief went on, turned around, and poured himself a cup of coffee.

He more or less shushed Chief H and sat back down. Leaders sometimes have tells — like poker players — except these tells indicate when they are becoming annoyed, irritated, or angry. Pretty sure that was his.

I completed my brief, took a breath, and looked to the Commander for feedback. He said, and I will never forget it, "I don't know how you did it, but I'm impressed."

Fuck, yeah. Suck it, Chief H.

The next morning, I was back in RGV Sector, at the gas pumps where we gassed up our government vehicles, waiting in line when a Tahoe pulled up behind me. I looked in my rear-view mirror, and who did I see? Chief H.

Bloody Hell—I really don't want to talk to this guy.

I tried to lean over toward the passenger side so he wouldn't see me, but too late. He opened his door and started walking up to my driver's side.

As he approached, I continued to pretend like I was doing something in my passenger seat and didn't notice him until he tapped on my window. Tap, tap, tap. Dammit. I acted surprised and pushed the button to roll down my window.

The first words out of his mouth were, "How do you think you did yesterday?"

I answered, "I was nervous at first but once I got in my groove"

He interrupted in what I can only describe as condescending and with a chuckle. "When you got in your groove? I don't think you got into a groove."

I interrupted back, "Well, the Commander said he was impressed."

Dick.

No, "hey, good job, you pulled it off, but maybe we can talk about improving your briefing skills."

No "congratulations, you did what neither the prior guy nor I could do." Just criticism. After I bit back, he laughed, said something, and walked back to his vehicle. Another lesson in the type of leader I would not be.

The moral of the story is this — **Don't be a dick**.

When you have an opportunity to lead people, show them you can lead, and that you care enough about them to provide help. Encouragement, training, anything except just criticism in their journey.

I have told this story repeatedly, and it brings back all those insecurities that I was dealing with at that time.

Thankfully, there were enough other good leaders: peers, my husband — always a valued mentor — and teammates around to help me during the times when I was unsure and learning. But it wasn't this guy.

I threw a lunch party for my team in celebration. I hadn't done this by myself. Without them, none of it would have been accomplished. They needed a win, and we just got a big one!

We carried on, proceeded to nail it every time we briefed, and became known as a high-performing team that I was told, at one point, was the area team that the other area teams should strive to emulate. Awesome!

I don't know if someone was just trying to blow smoke, but I took it and ran with it.

Chapter 11
Unexpected Allies

Another year and another promotion later, I was headed back to McAllen station, this time as the Deputy Patrol Agent in Charge (DPAIC) — second in command of the station. For all his faults, Chief H. promoted me 3 times in 3 years.

Maybe he was pressured to, maybe he had to hire a female (wink, nudge), I don't know. Challenge accepted.

And whoa, did I walk into a shit show.

McAllen had, over the last two years, become the number one apprehending station in the US Border Patrol. They also received hundreds of trainees during that period. The union and station management, (my new boss, the PAIC, but not the same guy who was there when I was an FOS) didn't see eye-to-eye on anything. And the union's answer to that situation was to formally file a grievance against management for just about everything. I was given my marching orders that I was to make nice with the union and fix that relationship.

The station detention area, never designed for the flow of people it was handling, was a source of extreme irritation for the union and management alike. And scabies. Yes, scabies — the people we took into custody were infested with them.

I arrived early, by 7 am, on my first day reporting for duty as the DPAIC — as I had done for just about any day shift my entire career. Around 8:30 am, I was notified that there as a woman dressed all in black standing at the front door of the station.

Our front desk staff was not in yet, so I went to the front door to see what she wanted. There stood a stout woman, decked out in all black, wearing a black ball cap, with the letters OSHA in large white block letters across the front of the hat.

You would have thought she was FBI waiting to do a raid the way she was dressed.

Ok, what was this about? I had not even had an opportunity to meet with the union, so I wasn't aware of the problems yet. But OSHA? What could they possibly be doing here?

Also, we're the government, you don't have any power here. Be gone before someone drops a house on you.

If you don't get the reference, put this book down right now and go watch the Wizard of Oz. You can thank me later.

OSHA primarily holds companies accountable for employee working conditions…and my employees work outside. In the field.

Ooooh…the detention area.

Sure enough, someone, likely the union, called OSHA regarding the terrible working conditions in the detention area. They weren't wrong. It was horrible. If you can imagine a sandstorm blowing into a building and covering everything in dust—multiply that by 10, and that was the level of dirt in and around the detention area. The HVAC system was never designed to handle the level of humans, dirt, you name it, that it was handling in this situation. The cleaning crew would come in, wipe things down, maybe once a day—but that wasn't enough either. It was not a sustainable situation.

The OSHA investigator interviewed me, and a bunch of other supervisors and agents related to the working conditions in the detention area. During the interview, she mentioned a notice they sent to the station months earlier.

I told her it was my first day, but I would ask around. I considered this a good thing because now maybe someone would listen and give us the help we needed to fix the situation. I did call the sector and they promptly came to the station. This is really when things started to take off with a resolution to the detention situation.

OSHA didn't actually have any enforcement power against another government agency. But they tried. They even attempted to get the local fire chief to shut us down for over-capacity. But again, they had no power over the Federal Government, and we had nowhere else to put people.

The fire chief wouldn't do it. He lived in the local area; he understood what was going on.

Every station in the sector was sharing the burden, as best that they could, and everyone was over capacity. At this point in time, people just started giving up—they would cross the river, walk to the nearest green and white truck or agent and turn themselves in. Much like what has been portrayed in the media today, there were often hundreds of people on the ground, out in the field waiting for transportation to the nearest station to begin processing.

However, the big take away is that because of this report to OSHA, RGV and McAllen station finally received the attention it needed.

A short time later, people started visiting, taking notice and at a national level, tried coming up with a solution. Nevertheless, once the Secretary finally came to visit and saw the mounds of dirt, tightly packed cells, and the fact that we had to keep the scabies-infested group of people outside (in what was supposed to be the Sally Port) —he finally declared a humanitarian emergency. That triggered some funding and help from FEMA, US Coast Guard's medical assistance, and so on.

Aside from the declaration from the Secretary of a humanitarian crisis, the Border Patrol finally received the funding to build a new, capable processing facility that would ultimately become the model for many sectors and similar facilities for years to come. This was the first time in my career when I started losing sleep over the job. This was when stress and anxiety would begin to become systemic, one hit right after another, like a drop of water on your forehead—not so bad at first, but eventually, torture. Over time, that takes a toll.

Your brain takes each hit, deals with it, but at a certain point doesn't have the time to calm back down and heal, so you end up in this constant state of hypervigilance waiting for the next ball to drop, or crisis situation. I began to not know what to do with myself if I wasn't dealing with an emergency—just waiting. I had pockets of stressful experiences that caused me occasional lack of sleep, but this was constant. I was beginning to really feel the stress.

I started taking over-the-counter PM medicines in order to, at least try, to sleep. It got to the point where I went to the doctor because I needed something to really knock me out.

I was afraid to take that stuff because it could be addictive, or I was afraid I wouldn't wake up if called, so I was very careful—but they didn't work anyway. I don't sleep well to this day. I still take over the counter PM medicine to help me get to sleep. I'm a work in progress.

My Lucky Charm

My boss, the new Patrol Agent in Charge (PAIC) of the station, was not good with public speaking—he didn't like it, he didn't want to do it. He was feeling the pressure from Sector and Washington, DC for all that was going on at our station. Everyone was. It seemed like every Friday there was some VIP from DC wanting a brief and a Border tour. This included Congressional representatives, their staffers, the DHS Secretary, Commissioner of CBP, Border Patrol executives and on and on. The Secretary of DHS decided he wanted to visit on Mother's Day—thanks, pal.

This was at the peak of the unaccompanied juvenile influx. We had a ton of unaccompanied juveniles in custody, and he and his wife thought it would be a nice gesture to visit them on Mother's Day. They didn't know who he was, or his wife, or that it was Mother's Day. People are ridiculous.

The Friday and weekly visits seemed to slow down a bit so my boss called me his lucky charm—fact was, he just wasn't present for them. I hosted the Secretary on Mother's Day so the PAIC could spend Mother's Day with his family. I have no words.

It was non-stop.

Instead of my PAIC handling these things, he started to conveniently have doctor's appointments on the same dates as these visits—every single time. Which left me, and my counterpart, the other DPAIC, to handle them. He *also* had doctor's appointments or some other excuse on the days we had to be at Sector for our weekly operational brief to the Chief and Deputy. We had a new Deputy come on board at this time, so more pressure to figure out who he was, what he was about, his expectations, how he liked to receive briefings and the types of questions he would ask.

I never felt fully prepared for those briefings; probably partly due to the fact that the PAIC was supposed to do them, and I would get thrown in at the last minute. More stress, and another not so great "leader" to not emulate in my future.

Funny story about my PAIC. He didn't go out in the field much—most PAICs don't have that luxury, so he would often be in his office on the computer. His office was about two doors down from mine, so I would often pass by on my way to detention, the bathroom, wherever—it was on the way to most parts of the station. He almost always had his door open.

He was a pretty small statured man, maybe 5'4. He was definitely shorter than me, and I'm not tall, maybe 5'6" with my boots on. However, he was masculine, if just miniature. Dark hair, with the classic mustache a lot of agents have. He had this big executive chair and almost always, he would be leaned back in the chair with his little legs just kicking away, a good foot off the ground. He couldn't touch the ground when he leaned back like that—always made me laugh.

Woo, that visual makes me chuckle thinking about it. It was like when a little kid sits in their dad's chair.

No hugs for you

Later that same year, RGV Sector held an award and promotion ceremony to recognize those who had been promoted within the last year and/or received awards. These are always nice events that family members are invited to, lots of photos are taken and memories codified.

My husband and I had been promoted within that time frame, so it was also a good opportunity for us to take some photos together in uniform. On stage, from right to left as you are looking at the stage, were Chief H, Deputy L and the master of ceremonies, Miss Irma. I don't remember what the process was, whether it was by station or rank or alphabetical, but several people had gone before me—most of the women giving a big hug to the Chief and the Deputy after shaking their hands.

Something about me, I'm not particularly physically affectionate, especially with people that I'm not either related to or really good friends with. I barely want to shake hands.

In fact, the pandemic was my ideal society. Everyone stayed 6 feet away, was afraid to touch anyone else and no one was on the roads or in the stores. I'd been preparing for that my whole life.

Nevertheless, in the Rio Grande Valley, and maybe throughout South Texas, people are very touchy-feely. I'm from New York, we say hello with a nod of the head and that'll do. We'd spent a good 10-15 minutes at the beginning of every meeting for everyone to go around and exchange pleasantries, hugs, handshakes, hellos and how is everyone before getting down to business.

I either really like or love you, have missed you—because I really like or love you or you're in a bad place and I'm comforting you in order to get a hug from me.

On stage, as I approached Chief H—who by this time you know is not my favorite person —he went in for the hand shake, which automatically shifted to a hug. I very quickly made eye contact with him, did a quick "no" shake of my head and awkwardly just stuck out my hand to shake and quickly pulled back. Hard pass on the hug.

After the promotion pinning, I was called up for another award — the Secretary's Award for the Corpus Christi ReCoM effort, which I was not expecting. Probably thinking that I was overcome with surprise as I approached him grinning widely, Chief H audibly said, "Do I get a hug this time?"

To which I shook my head and said, "No, I'd rather not," with a sarcastic half smile, and stuck out my hand again. Miss Irma caught it; she was very astutely observational.

He didn't put me in for the award anyway, my Coast Guard counterparts did. Hard pass again.

He wasn't there much longer after that — he retired. This thing happens to those in the Senior Executive Service (SES) in the Government when their bosses don't think they are doing their best or that they are not in the right place to best use their talents.

They receive a notification called a 3 R letter. One has three options upon receipt — **R**etire, **R**esign, or **R**elocate, thus the 3 Rs. It is a mechanism to reassign senior executives, but is more often used as a mechanism to get people out of a leadership position where they are no longer wanted or no one wants them in.

If the person receiving the letter does not want to relocate, they are forced to resign or retire. I can't say for sure that's what happened, since I wasn't in the right loop, but he retired without a lot of advanced notice, so that is my best guess.

Chapter 12
Labor/Employee Relations and Discipline

Maybe the worst 6 months of my career.

My first assignment in San Diego Sector was as an Assistant Chief Patrol Agent, and my area of responsibility included Labor Employee relations. Which spans everything from discipline to union relations and all the things in between. I would be involved in recommending and serving disciplinary actions on agents and employees, as well as union negotiations, grievances, hearing oral replies to disciplinary recommendations, working with specialists, legal counsel and so on.

It was an area that I was very interested in learning about, so I was fairly excited to get started. Plus, I had developed a good rapport and reputation with the union in RGV, where I had just left. That had to count for something, right?

Suffice it to say, it did not.

The upside to this position is you really learn your boundaries and rights as a manager. The downside to this position is that all you see all day long is the worst of the agency. Agents and employees who have done some pretty stupid things.

Just a few examples of some of the cases I handled are: DUI, drug use, Domestic Violence, Absence without Leave (AWOL) for days or weeks at a time — usually connected to alcohol abuse, alleged murder, marriage fraud, marriage to an illegal, lack of candor, any kind of EEO related violation, release of operational information...I mean, if you can think it, it came up.

I rarely got surprised at this point in my life by the things people did. I still felt disappointment, but rarely did anything surprise me.

One agent, literally fighting for his job, facing termination, showed up to his oral reply *high as a kite*. Alright, then. I had to remind myself that in the larger scheme of things, although it seemed daunting, this was a very small percentage of employees.

The majority of agents and employees stayed out of trouble and were morally sound.

The union president in San Diego at the time was a dude whose nickname really says it all — 'Jimmy, the Pimp.' He was a fairly senior agent, probably been around as long, or longer, than me in the agency. He worked his whole career in San Diego Sector, but I think he served at least at two different stations. By his account, he was a super-agent and his forte was highway work. He could pick a load car out of anywhere.

Although, he hadn't been in the field for years by this time.

He was arrogant, narcissistic, extreme right wing—all the things you think an extreme right-wing person is. I'm pretty sure they modeled the stereotype after this guy. He loved his nickname, thought it was hilarious. I don't know what happened to him in his career, but he essentially despised anyone in management, just because they were in management. As if managers hadn't also been field agents. I can only assume he got in trouble for something, fought the man and won, so he decided to take up the flag for the poor working agent and blame management for anything and everything.

He did not once ever come to a meeting looking to come to a resolution. He just wanted to fight.

His claim to fame when running for President of the union was that he would increase grievances, take everything to arbitration and win. He didn't win everything and taking everything to arbitration costs a lot of money…when you lose.

He claimed to have received something like 70% of the vote for the president position. Never mind that 30 people out of 2000 bargaining unit members ever voted. I am exaggerating those numbers, but you get the point, it's not far off.

As my work record had shown up to this point, I was pretty good at solving problems. Bringing people together and building consensus that was fair to all involved.

Man, would he challenge me in the months to come.

On one such occasion, we were meeting to discuss a grievance that one of the dispatchers filed over holiday time off. There was a severe shortage of dispatchers, so agents would often be assigned to perform those duties to supplement the shortage.

My team and I were seated on the far side of the conference table, with an exit door behind us and Jimmy and his team seated opposite of us. I was flagged on the left by one of my labor employee relation specialists and another agent on the right.

I'm not sure how the conversation devolved to this, but we ended up talking about why, or why not, agents should be performing the duties of a dispatcher. Jimmy's claim – and I apologize for the language—was and I quote, "Agents are too retarded to perform these duties."

Ok, number one, my granddaughter was diagnosed with down syndrome around this time, so I took particular offense to the term retarded.

Secondly, did you just categorically call the people you represent retarded?

I warned him, "Use that term again and this meeting is over."

As things got more heated, he continued to use the term, just ranting and yelling; I don't even think he heard me warn him. One of the other union representatives in the room (they always came with an entourage), was a bit more tempered in my experience. He was a big man. Jimmy wasn't big, per se, but he was middle age rounding, if you know what I mean.

This other guy was a big man, tall, probably 6'5", and towered over Jimmy, probably muscular in his earlier years, but nonetheless intimidating. But actually, a gentle giant.

This guy heard me warn Jimmy.

At the point where I had enough and was about to lose my cool, I stood up, Jimmy stood up and this guy stood up. He grabbed Jimmy by the shoulders, looking down at him, as Jimmy continued to rant, trying to get him to shut up.

I walked out of the room; my entourage followed me. I was pissed! This fucker got to me.

I collected myself in the hallway, with the help of my team. They did whatever they did to calm Jimmy down in the conference room. As we reentered several minutes later and took our seats, Jimmy didn't apologize. But he took it down a notch.

We resolved the grievance and I refused to discuss the other topic that day. It would have to be a discussion for another time. Have a great rest of your day everyone. Now, get out of my building.

One thing about labor employee relations is that during the time the agent is representing the union, they are more or less your equal in the scenario. Your rank or title doesn't mean a damn thing to them.

Meaning, they can be disrespectful and there's really no recourse.

Heated debate is fine, but straight up name calling and disrespectful language does not have to be tolerated. This was not the first and would not be the last frustrating meeting between the union reps of that time and me. They loved to pontificate and hear themselves talk.

Jimmy was eventually indicted for fraud.

He allegedly did some unsavory things with union funds. Karma, I love ya!

But it was still a miserable time. The same week the incident happened with the Peeper was my last week in this position. I was happy to hand it all over to my best bud, Dy.

Call me if you need anything, but also, don't call me. This shit show belongs to you now.

Chapter 13
The Best Job in the Border Patrol

Being a Patrol Agent in Charge (PAIC), the commander of a station is by far the best job in the Border Patrol. By the time I reached this position, May of 2016, I had done a lot of integration initiatives, strategic level work and the dreadful labor employee relations position.

However, that probably prepared me the best to take on this role as I would be developing a relationship with union representatives from my station and hopefully creating a partnership that would benefit the agents. Notable events during my tenure as the PAIC of Imperial Beach station included a corrupt agent's arrest, the Haunted Barn, and dealing with a wishful usurper.

The wishful usurper.

Before even beginning my tenure, I heard word that the person who had been acting in the PAIC position, Conor—who was also one of the station's deputies—was not at all happy with the fact that I was selected for the position.

I don't know that it was because it was me as a person—but I do know that it definitely had to do with the fact that he fully expected to be promoted into that position.

He was livid, in fact, and requested a meeting with the Chief of the Sector. He was one of those agents who was always friendly to my face, and I'd known of him in the past, but I'd never worked with him before. He was actually an incredibly intelligent and capable agent with a good reputation.

According to my sources, during the meeting with the Chief, he questioned the chief's judgement in selecting me for the position. But he was quickly cut off when the Chief told him, "She has been identified as a future leader in the organization and is being groomed for higher positions."

Ooh, fancy, I guess it was ordained, for lack of a better word.

I can only imagine how much this must have irritated Conor. I don't know what he thought he would gain from it; since it really only made him look like a whiney ass.

Knowing this had happened, my first day was a little awkward. I thought to myself—this isn't the first time I've walked into a role where people had doubts. Surely, I can win him over with my charm.

Yeah, not so much.

Conor was hilarious, jovial, and super fun to be around…to my face. I thought, 'Ah, thank God, I've won him over. We're good!' NOPE!

I had two deputies at the station—one for administrative functions and one for operations. The other Deputy, Don, and I got along famously. He was a very tenured agent and only about a year out from mandatory retirement. If I'm totally honest, he really helped to mold me as a PAIC. He turned out to be a great friend and partner.

As I was in my office one morning, after having been in the position for some time—I could hear chatter and scuttling about over in Conor's' office. The two deputies had offices just outside mine, to the left and right.

I could only wonder what they were talking about, so I proceeded to walk right into Conor's office unannounced—just as he was talking shit about me to Don and one of the senior Watch Commanders.

I stopped in my tracks as soon as I broke the plane of the door. They all just stared at me, looking like...OH SHIT! Little boys caught peeing in their mom's garden.

I immediately recognized what was going on and the complete silence as soon as I walked in surely confirmed that. I was shocked, hurt, and confused. Fuck you, guys.

Why were Don and the Watch Commander engaging in this conversation and not sticking up for me?

How often did this happen? What is this asshole saying about me to everyone?

I'd given him a lot of autonomy. I took his advice. I included him and the other deputy in decisions—there wasn't much else I could do to make it work.

I never did confront them about it—but I also never fully trusted any of them again. You never really know people. Don't get me wrong, I'm no angel; I said some unkind things about them in an email to my boss at one point, that I then inadvertently forwarded to them—please, may I have some crow for lunch? I tend to receive karma immediately for my stupid actions.

Twice during my tenure, Conor took off on long term details and I think the true reason was that he did not want to work for me.

It was honestly a relief because I needed a team and not a backstabber. He finally took a position on the northern border, and as far as I know, he is content and doing a good job. Good for him. I wish him the best, truly.

The Haunted Barn

Adjacent to the parking lot—but still within the compound of Imperial Beach Station—is the Sector's horse facility. For many, many years San Diego Sector hosted an event each Halloween called the Haunted Barn. Agents, the welfare and recreation association, and Border Patrol explorers (youth who are interested in a job in law enforcement) would create themed rooms throughout the horse stalls and guide folks through it as a haunted house. All proceeds went to charity.

This hadn't been done since the main organizer retired approximately 10-15 years ago.

One of my agents approached me and asked if we could bring it back.

I said, "Hell yeah – I love Halloween."

She, subsequently was the first agent I ever promoted to a supervisory position as a PAIC. I loved promoting people.

It was an incredible effort. Multiple stations from throughout the Sector participated. We decided to add a little spice to the mix and made the decorating theme a competition. After folks went through the different themed areas, they would vote on their favorite one. The station or team that got the most votes received the coveted Grim Reaper Trophy—fashioned out of metal by one of our very talented agents.

We marketed the event throughout the community, charging one canned good as the price for admission for two nights of Haunted Barn awesome-ness. All proceeds would be donated to the San Diego foodbank.

The first night was military and law enforcement appreciation night and only open to those folks, while the second night would be open to the general public. It was a legitimate spooky haunted house. The creativity and quality of effort was astounding, to be honest. We had themes ranging from zombies, reaching out and grabbing legs, to a meat factory—with a real beating heart and clowns...*shiver.* Clowns like Pennywise, not the ones at your kid's birthday. Which, frankly, also creep me out.

The first night we had around 700 people come through.

The line was about an hour and a half wait, but so worth it—as per attendees. The second night was even bigger.

We ended up collecting over 1500 canned goods, and I'm sure not every person in every family brought their own can—we didn't really keep track. We figured by the end we probably had 1500-2000 people come through in only two days.

The return of the Haunted Barn was a resounding success.

I played the part of the wicked witch, although I consider myself a good witch (wink, wink) —fitted with a harness (gear provided by our special operations folks) to fly in and startle the crap out of each and every group that entered the barn. We brought people through in groups of about 6 and the first thing they encountered when the door shut behind them was a real, live flying witch. Time after time, they let me loose, flying down right in front of the group, cackling away. It was SO. MUCH. FUN. I was hoarse and bruised the next day — so someone else took that role for the second night.

We did it again the following year, but could not make it work the third year. Traffic in the area had increased exponentially. I was in the Division Chief role by that time and we really had to focus on our actual jobs.

We had a good run bringing it back, if only for a few years. Great memories and we got to give back to the community in the process.

Corruption and Betrayal.

Around mid-point through my first year in the PAIC role, an agent who was detailed to the FBI task force called me one morning and asked if we could meet somewhere privately.

I was like, what the hell is this about?

He said he would let me know when we met, but that it was not good.

This FBI taskforce investigated corruption, but that hadn't quite clicked just yet. I met him in the parking lot of a grocery store. He approached my vehicle in plain clothes and hopped up into the passenger seat. He asked me if I recognized a name, Noe something. I don't remember his last name.

I said, no not specifically. I didn't know all 300 agents at the station by name and, typically, if I did know an agent by name by this point it was for one of the two reasons: they were in trouble or they were an incredibly exceptional agent. Usually, the former. He proceeded to tell me that the FBI had an informant who reported that this agent was smuggling drugs on duty.

The agent, when working certain locations, would wait for someone to toss a backpack over the border, go pick it up and deliver to his contact after shift.

My head was about to explode with anger, betrayal, and disbelief. I didn't know what to say. I remember looking down and thinking, that mother fucker. Good agents hate nothing more than a dirty agent—how dare you betray your fellow agents, your country, your oath?

Normally, we (at the BP leadership level) aren't brought into these situations or conversations until the investigating agency is ready to make an arrest. In this situation, they needed a bit more proof.

We worked with the FBI to set up cameras in the area reported to have been used for the criminal activity. Come to find out, it was an area we did not have camera coverage. A blind spot. A small canyon that was just outside the viewshed of the BPs existing camera suite. The agent knew this, of course, having worked the area for years—he knew exactly what the cameras could see and couldn't see and used that to his advantage.

I had to keep this quiet. I wasn't allowed to tell my deputies what was going on, but I was able to bring one other person into the fold so that we could assist the FBI in getting their proof.

The person I was allowed to bring in was one of my Special Operations Supervisors, Joe.

For a few weeks, Joe would come into my office, we'd close the door and he would brief me on the progress made to get the proof the FBI needed.

Now, my deputies were no dummies. They knew something was up and every time Joe would leave my office, Don would be outside his office with the same question, "What's going on?"

"Nothing," I'd say and walk back into my office.

I am a horrible liar. I couldn't let him see my face.

The FBI shortly got their proof, but we had to arrange for the arrest of the agent. I made a few things very clear: they would not arrest him in the field and they would not parade him through the station after his arrest as had been done in the past with agent arrests. They agreed.

I could finally read my deputies into the situation, so I called them into my office and explained what was going on. Don told me, "I was getting pissed, not knowing what was going on and being left out", but now he understood.

I came up with an elaborate plan to keep Noe in the dark, as well as the rest of the agents, about what was going to transpire on D-day. We also had to find a way to get him unarmed, without him being the wiser so when they confronted him for the arrest, there would be less risk.

The FBI had their warrant and had to make the arrest by a certain time to get him arraigned the next morning.

Noe was working day shift. Joe put out an email that there was a mix up with weapons and serial numbers, and we needed to check every single day-shift agent's weapon before they went home that day. We called in agents, one by one, throughout the shift. They would unload their weapon before entering the station, report to Don's office—he'd check the serial number and they would be on their way. Noe was the absolute last agent called in—just around 3:30 pm. Day shift ran from 6 am to 4 pm.

He emptied his weapon outside the station and was escorted to Don's office by Joe. My office door was closed as I was in contact with the Chief to let him know when the deed was done. I was usually at the gym by this time in the day so it was normal for my door to be closed.

As Noe walked toward Don's office, I heard Don say, "Oh hey, Noe, come on in." So, he did.

As soon as he entered the office, the three FBI agents waiting inside converged on him from all sides and made the arrest—put him in handcuffs, without issue. I let the Chief know it was done and opened my door. I had a private entrance to my office, from the parking lot—through which the FBI agents escorted Noe to their waiting vehicle and took him away.

If you ever need me to plan a surprise, just let me know. I'm pretty good at it.

We had also told the day shift Watch Commander that the PAIC (me) needed to address all day shift agents about some discrepancies with time and attendance so they would need to report for a post shift muster that day. That was a ruse. I wanted to address them and tell them what had just happened—before they heard it either on the news or from some other source. Don and Conor accompanied me to the post-shift muster.

This was the shift from which Noe came. He had friends and colleagues on this shift.

The agents weren't super happy they were being held up from leaving. As I walked into the muster room, the entire shift was as far back in the room as possible. It was typical for the senior agents to line up against the back wall, with all the younger agents up front. What I saw was straight up irritation, until I came clean and delivered the news.

I'm not one to mince words, so I told them Noe was just arrested by the FBI for smuggling drugs; he was dirty, and he gave away the farm in the process. Come to find out, Noe had shared all of the operational intelligence he had with the "lady friend" he had gotten mixed up with during his little tryst. We call this a honey trap. The bad guys now knew every hole we had in surveillance, every section of the border that wasn't covered. They. Knew. Everything.

The response from the shift was visceral, angry, and absolute betrayal. Noe was a "good agent," a hard worker, but lately he kept asking to have his assignment changed, saying he was tired or had a rough night—when, really, he needed to be in a particular area to receive his shipment. The agents really had a hard time believing it.

As the agents spouted off a bit, Don cut in and said, "Hey – this is hard on all of us. I just had to watch one of our agents, wearing the same uniform as me, get handcuffed and arrested by the FBI. It was like seeing my own son getting arrested." Ouch. That touched some nerves, but shut them down.

As I continue to see and say, you never really know people. Noe was eventually tried, convicted, and terminated from employment. I enjoyed that one.

An agent approached me after muster broke and said, "No one's ever done that."

'Done what?' I wondered.

He said, "Through his whole career, whenever something like this happened—they never really knew what happened, the ground truth. Agents got whatever information they got from the news and rumor mills." He appreciated that I was open and transparent and felt an obligation to inform my agents myself. I thought, maybe I am doing something right as a leader. It was good to get positive feedback—validating, actually.

I spent a little over 2 years in that position. It was hard to leave, but I felt like I left an overall positive mark during my time there.

Chapter 14
Leadership is lonely

It is common, albeit unfortunate, in any organization that as you move up the ladder, you have fewer and fewer peers, friends and people you can genuinely talk to, share things with and have candid conversations.

People don't come to your office to see how your day is going. There is almost always a reason and it's usually in the form of a problem. It is just the reality.

I haven't made many true, close friends, honestly, since middle school. My childhood best friend is still my best friend and soulmate and I am certain we will be Thelma and Louise-ing it up in our nursing home days.

I have acquaintances and a few folks I could call friends, but there are only about 3 people I've met as an adult that I routinely spend time with, besides my family. I'm an introvert, it's ok. I keep my circle small; I don't have the energy for anything bigger.

I sincerely enjoy silence and alone time. I know I've found someone who will stick when, even after we've spent time apart or don't talk for extensive periods of time, we pick up right where we left off. They always make time for me and me for them.

Mary Margaret, my BP Academy roommate, Autumnal Pancakes (aka Autumn), the chic who told me I intimidated her and Dy — my work BFF. I know these chickadees would be among those bringing the shovels with no questions asked if I ever called.

Mary Margaret

Mary, the slender red head who I shared living space and bonded with during our initiation into the US Border Patrol. Mary and I connected immediately — probably because she is an extrovert and not afraid to talk to anyone.

And she was handing me a beer after a very long day.

Mary is vivacious, full of life and art. She is cultured and intelligent. I got my first pedicure with Mary and I thought, oh, ok, this is how the cultured people live, I like it. I remember one evening, as we were all pre-gaming before we headed out, she and one of our classmates put on a little show in the hallway — singing songs from the musical Grease. She was certainly not shy.

Sharing the academy experience is something unexplainable. She struggled in Spanish and I struggled in law, initially, so we helped each other out supplementing each other's deficiencies. We both loved a good Saturday night out at the Irish bar in downtown Charleston, Tommy Condon's. Ah, the good ole days, when neither of us had any real-life responsibility, except to ourselves. Just two single red heads living it up in Charleston, S.C, making more money than either of us had probably ever had up to that point.

Every Saturday, and we were there EVERY Saturday, the live band at Tommy Condon's would play the Unicorn song to close out the night; an Irish folk song about how unicorns got left off Noah's Ark. Mary and I would join in, doing all the animal hand imitation movements, singing along with the music — green alligators and long neck geese, humpty-back camels and chimpanzees. Some cats and rats and elephants, as sure as you're born, but the loveliest of all is the unicorn — I'm singing it in my head right now.

The Macarena was big during this timeframe too. I was asked (as if I had a choice) to lead my PT class in the Macarena as we warmed up for swimming one morning, instead of the typical calisthenics. One of the instructors had seen us out over the weekend and thought it would be funny to have me lead the class in the Macarena. Pretty sure it was that Diablo guy. Fuck it, I thought I owned it.

Anyway, Mary and I would crawl back in the transport van the academy provided at the end of the night to transport us back to the base. This was after we almost always had to jump over a hip height wall leaving the bar to get to wherever our ride was picking us up. Oh Lord, it was a sight to behold. Neither one of us made it look pretty. We were well known to almost always be together.

However, we didn't usually sit together on the bus to firearms. The firearms range was offsite, so we had to take a bus to get there and I always sat with Jack. Jackie-poo, as Mary and I dubbed him.

Mary loves to tell this story.

One day, as I stepped up onto the bus and was looking for Jack to sit next to—someone had the audacity to already be in the seat, having taken MY spot next to Jack. As Mary tells it, I stared this person down, making them as uncomfortable as possible, laser focused into their soul, until they got the picture.

"Uh, do you want to sit here?" Yeah, I do. No one sits with Jackie-poo but me! I guess I can be intimidating.

Once we left the academy, we stayed in pretty close contact. Over time, those contacts became less frequent, but never stopped. Either one or both of us experienced the loss of child, getting married, having more children, divorce, life's ups and downs.

Mary left the Border Patrol to pursue a much higher calling after both of her children were diagnosed with autism. She returned to school to get her degree in that field and now works as an advocate, trainer, boss lady, and a super mom who understands what her kids, who are becoming adults, need. She has built an amazing career and reputation for herself.

As I mentioned earlier, we started doing a girls' trip every year or two, about 8 or so years ago. We just planned our next one — watch out Disney World, Mary and Kathy are coming for mom-cation part IV. Mary makes me laugh and I make her laugh and we both need that.

Autumnal Pancakes (aka Autumn)

Miss Autumn occupied a cubicle across from my husband during our first stint at Headquarters, 2007-2010 timeframe. She was a contractor providing some sort of professional services support. Whenever I went over to visit my husband or grab him for lunch, I'd notice her, a pretty young girl sitting next to my husband, but she never really spoke to me. We probably said a courteous 'hi' to each other. I'm not one to make the first move.

My husband mentioned at some point that I should get to know her — he was always trying to find me friends (wink). I found out later, that she was trying to figure out a way to approach me, introduce herself, perhaps, and apparently, I intimidated the hell out of her. I didn't mean to. I don't think I'm intimidating, but that damn RBF.

One day as I was standing outside my husband's cubicle, she was going on about something that happened on the bus ride to work and trying to think of the name of a song and as Autumn did, she started singing part of it — I'm pretty sure there is a musical to her life playing in her brain at all times. I recognized the song and said, "Oh yeah, it's (whatever it was, I can't remember) by Trick Pony."

That was it: we chatted, clicked and connected. She is also very inappropriate, hilarious and sarcastic—she should have been a Border Patrol Agent. Over the years, whenever I came back to DC for any type of work trip, we would always find time to get together. She's a solid rock of a friend, even if she gives too much of herself sometimes.

Dy

Dy and I are very different, but we balance and complement each other. She is creative and has a million "brilliant" ideas a day, whereas I am practical, methodical and always seem to shoot a hole in her ideas—err, I mean, give her realistic expectations. We endured a lot of pressure and crisis from work over the years, particularly as two outspoken female leaders with fearless attitudes while dealing with the misogynistic culture that unfortunately still exists in pockets throughout the organization.

Dy and I both started out as agents in Nogales. Dy came in about 3 years after I did. She worked for my husband on his work unit for and we sat together at a wedding we both attended in Las Vegas for a co-worker. I was with my husband and Dy brought her cousin. Her cousin, yeah, right.

I was a bit clueless. I didn't know nor did I care that Dy is a lesbian. So, when she introduced her cousin, I bought it, hook, line and sinker. Although it was early 2000s, she wasn't comfortable being out yet. That was her business.

I left Nogales in 2004, moved to Erie, PA and subsequently ended up at Headquarters in Washington, DC in 2007. Dy came up to HQ sometime between 2007 and 2010, because we would occasionally see each other and I had heard she was taking a position up there. We still didn't get to know each other during this timeframe. It wouldn't be until 4 or 5 years later, when we both ended up in San Diego Sector that we finally connected.

Dy and I bonded over the stupidity of the people around us, mansplaining, our common affection for furry critters and our preference for them over people. Also, sarcasm, lots and lots of sarcasm. Our families would become very close, spending holidays in each other's company, supporting each other through life's trials and tribulations, both personal and work related. Dy and I were the only two female Patrol Agent's in Charge in San Diego Sector at the same time, and eventually she would follow suit and take over a few positions I vacated as I promoted up and out of San Diego. She surpassed all expectations, from others and frankly, herself in becoming the first female Chief of San Diego Sector.

While I was serving as the Division Chief of Operations in San Diego Sector, the commander of all the station and field commanders, I held weekly meetings where I required each station commander to report in person to headquarters. The prior Division Chief held meetings, but they were held at a different location each time. The new Deputy didn't want it done this way any longer, and neither did I, frankly.

I was a bit younger than most of the Commanders, and a woman (the first woman to hold this position in the nation), and not organic to San Diego. I was an implant. Much like RGV Sector, the majority of San Diego agents started there and never left. Most of the station Commanders during this time, except for Dy and maybe one

162

other, started in San Diego and promoted through the ranks there with few of them ever leaving. Or if they did, they came right back.

The way they did things was the best and only way to do them, just ask them. They held their own "commander meetings" – invitation only (I never got an invite, even when I was Commander of Imperial Beach, and their peer) – a shadow leadership consortium if you will, and I was essentially brought in to do what I do: bring people together, and instill process and accountability. Bring some team to the team. A particular group of leaders were known throughout the sector as the "coffee club" so a few of my peers and I (Dy, included) created our own anti-coffee club coffee club.

The Division Chief position is not a job most people seek out. It is not easy wrangling 11 Type A personalities. They were kings over their kingdoms. It may actually be the worst job in the Border Patrol; on par with the labor relations position.

I threw my name in the hat when the announcement came out, but was relieved when they closed the list without selecting. Far fewer people applied than the Chief desired, so they closed the list and announced it again hoping for a better turnout, application-wise.

When they announced it again, I didn't apply because I didn't necessarily want the job. The Chief asked me if I had applied this time and I told him no. I was annoyed that if he wanted me for the position in the first place, then why didn't he hire me off of that last list? I was happy being a station commander.

My husband and I had every intention of leaving California as soon as we could after our daughter graduated high school, and I think she was junior around this timeframe. I didn't think it was fair of me to take a position I knew I wasn't going to stick around too long for. I also had it pretty good. I had the autonomy to be there for my daughter and for all of her events: soccer, choir, theater, chaperoning, you name it. I sacrificed time with her when she was younger and doesn't remember it, but this was the time in her life she would remember and I made it clear that she was my priority.

However, I was afraid of who I may have to work for if I didn't put in, and the Chief encouraged me to apply. So, I caved. I only really had one true competitor to the position and he was eventually hired as my direct peer in another Division Chief position at the Sector. So, here I was, feeling woefully unprepared for what was ahead of me — catching a theme?

During one of my first all-hands commander's meeting, one of the tenured commanders, a balding man quickly approaching mandatory retirement age of 57, but still in pretty good physical shape, was griping about some change initiative. He got loud, he complained on one side of the issue and then also complained about the other side of the issue.

I just let him go, staring into his eyes in utter disbelief as he continued. When he finished, I was bewildered.

I paused a minute and then I asked him if he realized he just spoke out of both sides of his mouth. I have a knack for keeping my cool, particularly when I know someone is trying to get a rise out of me. People have told me that it is one of the traits they admire about me.

In fact, I lower my voice in these types of situations, rather than meeting them at their level. My RBF is my armor. Remember, we don't cry. Feelings is the other 'F word' and I would not allow these guys to see me crack.

Dy, on the other hand, had no RBF game whatsoever. She can, but didn't on this day.

Dy and I could not, should not, sit next to each other at meetings —and it was even worse if we sat anywhere within eye shot of each other though. Too many shenanigans. During that meeting, as the same tenured commander carried on about something else, Dy sat directly across the table from me. I made the mistake of looking over at her.

Her face was contorted up horribly, her mouth hanging open, like she was seeing a train wreck happen right in front of her and there was nothing she could do to stop it. I swear I could hear her thoughts— "You are a special kind of stupid, aren't you?"

It was all I could to do to maintain my composure and not bust out laughing.

I immediately texted her, "Fix your face." She managed it.

She'd have to fix her face many times to come. We tried to behave, but it was really too easy not to. There was so much fuel for the sarcasm fire.

Chapter 15
Becoming a Mentor – However Unintentional

In part and parcel to the realization that as a woman, moving up the ranks in a male dominated profession, I was being watched, I was also seen as a role model. Whether or not I wanted it. I realized that I have a lot to share, and I wanted to be the change that I would like to have seen.

Much like everything about my generation (Gen X, if you're wondering), we overcorrected to be and provide all the things we felt like we needed and didn't get. Millennials and Gen Z are our doing—we created them, there I said it.

I was climbing steps, setting history, blazing trails and doing things differently than had been done before me. I thought I was just doing my thing—trying to make decisions that I could sleep with at night. I still tried to hold on to the fantasy that I wasn't a 'female agent,' dammit, I was *just an agent*.

But I wasn't *'just an agent,'* for a lot of reasons, least of which was being female. I had to accept this and then use it for good.

It wasn't until other people started telling me that I was different than any leader they had before that I really took stock of my actions. I took to heart and put into practice the leadership training I received, and the feedback we got from our subordinates and peers during those courses. I worked hard to be the leader that my people needed me to be at any given time.

I wasn't always that way. And I didn't always succeed. When I first promoted, things were black and white. Over time, I came to know that not everything is black and white. Different types of people need to receive different types of leadership.

In the latter part of my career, I had the opportunity and honor to participate on panels or interviews, and I actually loved it. Panels on leadership, women in law enforcement leadership and mentoring. You'd think I'd go 'Eek, public speaking' — but it turns out this type of public speaking doesn't make me as nervous. It also turns out I have some shit to say!

Women in particular, but also men, started to seek me out as a mentor. One of my longest mentoring relationships is with a man — and not a Border Patrol Agent. He does work for CBP — but it was a random pairing. CBP created a mentoring portal wherein you could sign up to mentor or be mentored. This young man found me and we've been chatting once a month for over two years.

I thoroughly enjoy mentoring. I participated as a mentor several times for the same CBP Leadership Institute training from where I got certified several years before. I loved it. I love to share my experiences, my wisdom (when did I become wise? I have no clue), advice with people and then even more, I love to see them succeed.

Not necessarily because of me, but I hope I maybe had some small part in helping them get over the hump. Mentoring was an opportunity to help people, which was the reason I originally wanted to get into Law Enforcement. Helping people in this way was not exactly what I had in mind in my 20's, but it is what my career evolved to.

Adjutants

Although at times lonely, being an executive in the Border Patrol does have its benefits and privileges. One such benefit was that you were afforded an adjutant.

An adjutant comes from military practice where a staff officer in the Army, Air Force, or Marine Corps. assists the commanding officer, and is responsible especially for correspondence. In the Border Patrol, their role was expanded to include maintaining their principal's calendar, travel arrangements, traveling with their principal, being a gatekeeper of their principal's time and energy, and just generally making sure the principal had what they needed daily for each task that day. These folks are typically high performers at the first line and higher supervisory level. They have proven themselves to rise above their peers in a number of ways. They compete for and are selected to perform the duties of an adjutant on a very competitive basis. It is a challenging role. I was an adjutant earlier in my career, during my first tour at HQ, which I mentioned earlier.

These folks are afforded the opportunity to really learn what upper-level leadership does, deals with, and how government really works. They get to be in the room where the hard decisions are made.

Adjutants and their principles become very close. They become confidantes to their principals and vice versa—you spend a lot of time with your adjutant. More time than you spend with your family. It's critical that they know their principal personally and what their priorities are.

My last adjutant and I spent the night together at the Dallas airport. She made me snack packs whenever we would travel because, for *some* reason, I'm scared to not have food available in case

I get hungry at any given moment. Adjutants become very protective of their principals because they see them as they truly are...*almost human*. They are the one person that I could share my most honest thoughts with. I wanted to know their opinion of topics discussed, interactions, and their ideas. I made them a part of the team. They see you at your worst, and they see you at your best. These folks get exposure to the inner workings of the agency, and also get exposure for themselves as future leaders.

This relationship makes it not quite so lonely. I specifically chose females to serve as my adjutants. Let me explain why.

I had two male adjutants and they were both great! No issues. However, they were in place when I came into the positions for which they were serving a principal who left. As a woman who people are watching, I did not want to give anyone any fodder for rumors. I think I mentioned earlier that if you want anyone to know anything, just tell a Border Patrol Agent—it will spread like a July fire in California.

A woman with a male adjutant, and also a man with a female adjutant, will undoubtedly, at one point or another, be accused of having an inappropriate relationship. Wrong, right, or indifferent, people gossip. I can't tell you how many times I've dispelled rumors I heard about other people, or myself. UGH! Nothing worse to derail a career than this type of rumor.

I also wanted to give female agents the adjutant opportunity. There are more men in leadership positions than women and most of them chose male agents as their adjutants — probably for the same reason I chose women. They didn't want people spreading rumors about them, or often times their significant other did not approve — so that further limits opportunities for female leaders in the organization.

You may wish it wasn't true, but it's one of those very harsh realities.

Both of the women I had as adjutants promoted out of the position either directly or shortly after returning to their sectors. Liz and Rose. I am so proud of them.

They took the chance on the opportunity — not knowing if it would benefit their careers or if they even wanted to take it on, but they were awesome and I consider both of them true friends to this day. For both, the opportunity gave them some insight into the agency and reignited a desire in them to go further and do more. I can't wait to see their future successes.

Chapter 16
Focus on Things You Can Change

Around the time I became the Division Chief of Operations in San Diego, this one feeling started nagging at me.

I just didn't want to do this anymore.

I was running the same rat race over and over again, day after day of one operational crisis after another. Actually, the same operational crisis over and over again. How did we keep ending up at the same damn place? Oh yeah, it's the way we've always done it. GRR.

Well, that ain't workin! We were in constant crisis mode — even when things weren't a real crisis, the pressure from on high made it a crisis. Mind you, the Border Patrol is very good at operational crisis response. It wasn't hard, but it was exhausting.

One particular Saturday, on my day off — as if that was really a thing — I was attempting to enjoy an outing with my family at a place similar to a Dave and Buster's, but smaller. I was looking forward to getting in the batting cages and working off some stress.

I never left home without my work phone, because God forbid, something happened and I couldn't be reached. I was in a position that really had no back up, no peer — the business end of a funnel. Information went from the field, to me, to my Deputy or Chief, and then to HQ. Or HQ would contact me directly. I literally could not miss a phone call. My work phone was the proverbial ball and chain.

I would tell my people and my boss before going into a movie — I'm going to be in a movie for a few hours, give me a minute to call you back if you call.

Anyway, the Deputy Chief of Operations from HQ had emailed earlier for some data, so I delegated to one of my folks to get the data together. It wasn't easy data to collate, so it was taking some time. He was receiving pressure from his boss, so that pressure rolled downhill to me.

Here I am, a pretty responsive person, never miss a call, an email, anything. I'm working on it, and this boss says to me via text, "I don't think you understand the critical nature of this request."

I think I do. This is not a real crisis, buddy. Take it down a notch. No one is dead, dying, or in critical condition on their way to the hospital, so your lack of preparation is not my crisis. I'm trying to have a rare day with my family and this…really? This is how you're going to converse with me. I didn't have a lot of respect for this guy.

It didn't help my attitude that this same guy, 15 or so years earlier, when I was a first line supervisor involved in recruiting, was the HQ Assistant Chief that I had the unmitigated GALL to email directly with a question about recruiting.

He asked my supervisor, "Who does she think she is? A first line supervisor directly emailing an Assistant Chief at HQ?"

Pardon me, I thought we both put our pants on one leg at a time. MMM — You are a tool.

Needless to say, I wasn't sleeping well during this time — I don't think I had slept well since 2007.

I remember telling a colleague about a dream I had. I was on duty, in a field—a field I had actually traversed as an agent and recognized in my dream. There were all these baby rattle snakes coiled up all around me and all of a sudden, they started springing up, coming at me, one after the other.

This was my life—and now my dreams.

Side note—this was a real-life field scenario I had experienced, except for the baby rattlesnakes jumping up to strike. The other agents and I, upon realizing we were surrounded, more or less tip-toed our way back to pavement side stepping coiled up rattlesnakes. YIKES. Thankfully it was a cool morning.

I would stand at my desk (I had acquired one of those fancy standing desks—God, save my back), answering email after email, taking phone call after phone call from HQ. Them trying to understand and control operations from 30,000 feet and 3000 miles away, meanwhile, an agent is in true crisis somewhere suffering from PTSD or depression or worse, and I thought —I do not want to fucking do this anymore. I'm tired. You should have promoted me when I was younger and had more energy.

Most people at the most upper echelons of the agency don't last more than 2 years in those positions. It's too much and frankly, they've already had a full career, been battle tested and just gotten bruised for it.

Chapter 17
Leaving the Border Patrol:
Changing Roles and Expectations.

I hit my 20 years in 2016, guaranteeing my law enforcement retirement eligibility. But I couldn't actually retire, because I came in so young, until I had *25 years* in. The rule of thumb was this: retire with 20 years if you're 50 or older or retire at any age with 25 years in.

I worked too long and too hard to walk away from that. I could do this, but I really didn't want to. It was not fun anymore.

It was 2019, and my daughter graduated high school that June. I had turned down a few opportunities to move on or up — one being for the Deputy Chief in Tucson Sector.

I would have loved to be able to go back to the Sector I started at, but the timing just wasn't right. Additionally, locations where my husband and I could work and live in the same household were few and far between. We could stay where we were — where he was in the neighboring sector, El Centro, or we could go to HQ.

We could have made a Yuma/El Centro split work, but both he and I had promoted beyond any opportunities available at those sectors at that time.

He was the Deputy Chief in El Centro, Acting as the Chief at that time. Any other sectors would be too far from each other for either of us to have a reasonable commute and we refused to live in different households. We'd seen it done and it rarely turned out well. We decided that Washington, DC for another tour would be our best bet.

We both really wanted to get out of California—too expensive and always on fire. Our house had been one ridge away from getting caught up in a raging wildfire just the summer before. So, it was time to go.

I got picked up first and made the move ahead of him. HQ leadership had plans for me. Little did they know, I had plans for me too—I was planning my exit strategy.

I found a job announcement for a Senior Executive position that was just up my alley: Executive Director for the Planning, Analysis and Requirements Evaluation (PARE) Directorate, in another component of CBP called Operations Support (OS). This would not be in the Border Patrol, and it was not a law enforcement covered position. I figured out that I didn't need to stay in a law enforcement position until I hit 25 years. You only need 20 years covered to qualify for the law enforcement retirement rate—which is only slightly more than regular government retirement by 0.7% or something. Beyond that, no matter how long you stay in a law enforcement position after the initial 20 years, you only get 20 years LEO covered credit toward your retirement. Any time beyond that is calculated at the regular government retirement rate.

I applied for the job. You can't win if you don't play. Border Patrol leadership was expecting me to put in for the National level Deputy Chief of Operations, and I did—just in case I didn't get this other job. They put me in the position in an acting capacity only a few months after I came back up to headquarters and I did my damn best.

COVID hit during that time and Title 42 was executed — allowing US officials to immediately expel anyone who entered the US illegally during the pandemic. We rallied and took care of business, all the while, I'm secretly (or not — nothing is a secret in the Border Patrol) interviewing 3 different times for this other executive-level position.

After the third interview and every indication I was going to be selected, I finally caved and told the Deputy Chief of the Border Patrol. Incidentally, the same person who was the Chief in San Diego and had hired me for the Division Chief position there.

I don't think anyone ever expected this from me. He didn't, but he supported people leaving to get other experiences and become more well-rounded to bring their experiences back to the BP. I didn't know if I would be back.

After I entered on duty in the new job, I got rid of all but 5 of my uniforms — just in case. But it was official. I was going civilian.

I would have to figure out how to communicate without using a curse word as a comma.

Over my career, I moved Sector duty locations 5 times, back and forth across the country and from one border to the other. I held multiple positions in each of the Sectors, took three long-term details to other Sectors or agencies, and experienced multiple shifts in the political landscape of the United States, as well as the impact the shifts took on the organization, and the people within it.

Every 2-3 years in the 27 years I was in service, the national level Chief changed, not to mention the changes at Sector and station levels. The running joke at most stations was, if you don't like the new guy, just wait them out. Leaders don't stick around for long. The only constant is change.

Misogynists wear nice ties.

I spent 18 months as the Executive Director over PARE. The person who hired me retired, about 8 months after I came on. *Her* boss had moved on and she wasn't promoted to his position, so I think she felt like it was time to go.

So, we had a whole new leadership team coming in.

The new Deputy, who would be my direct supervisor, had worked for CBP International Affairs in the past. He was voted off the CBP island a few years before and went to the Citizenship and Immigration Service. He was brought back because someone felt like he wasn't treated fairly at that time and had served on the presidential transition team so he deserved another chance, blah, blah, blah. He spent most of his career in the Department of State, before coming to CBP.

He was a diplomat. He used diplomacy, as it were, more than once on me. Answering a straight question without a straight answer. Not saying no, but meaning no, was his usual tactic.

We didn't start great and it only digressed from there. The woman who served in this position prior to him warned me about him before she left. She worked with him in the past and knew his reputation. I would learn exactly what she meant very shortly.

She brought me on, knowing and appreciating what I had already done and accomplished throughout my career. She trusted me. She gave me assignments and tasks to help me grow. Some of those things were arguably things she didn't necessarily want to do, or that were not really meant for her "level" and a newer executive should get some experience in.

One of those tasks was serving as the executive representative for the Component's budget. I did not have much experience with formulating or executing federal budgets. It was a definite gap in my experience. I was somewhat eager to learn, but also quite intimidated by it. Suffice it to say, the federal budget process is very archaic and confusing.

Very soon after the new Deputy arrived, he came by my office to introduce himself. The very first words out of his mouth were: "How did you get an office with a window? I don't have a window."

Umm, ok. Hi.

"This is the office they gave me," I responded. He then proceeded to find our logistics person to find out why he didn't have an office with a window. I was thinking, is this guy going to make me move out of this office so he can have a window? Glad to see your priorities are in order.

This was going to be interesting. Nice to meet you, I guess.

How do I describe this man? He was thin, though not gaunt, physically fit, with perfect posture. Graying, but with a full head of nice hair, round eyeglasses — the studious looking type. His suit was obviously not a cheap one and his tie was neatly tied in a double Windsor knot (I'm full of crap — I have no idea what a double Windsor is). He looked uppity, but professional, if not a little pretentious. He was very proper in his demeanor and speech, but always just a hint of condescension. He was what you call 'a picture-perfect diplomat.'

Shortly thereafter, he scheduled a meeting to discuss my directorate, find out what we did and what I was responsible for.

I was very friendly towards him and explained some of my projects and assignments — what my divisions were responsible for, and so on. I mentioned that I was the Executive representative for the budget process.

He made a face, not a nice one. Maybe a confused face.

He asked, very condescendingly, "Why are YOU doing that? That's the Deputy's responsibility. I did that when I was at CIS."

I felt like I had been caught doing something I wasn't supposed to and sheepishly answered that it was a gap for me and the prior Deputy thought it would be a good idea that I got some experience in that area. He shook his head as if in understanding.

Look dude, I'm not trying to take anything away from you, it was given to me.

We chatted for a bit until he said, "You seem very direct," but with a very *'don't you think you're special'* tone.

I am very direct and I may have said that — but I do usually warn people.

I'm not sure what I did or said, but it didn't seem like he was giving me a compliment. I mean, I was nervous — this was my new boss, I didn't want to sound stupid or like I didn't know what my own work was. I thought I was exhibiting confidence; maybe I was a little more animated than usual. I did have a lot of coffee that morning.

So, he was going to take my office and he was going to take the budget stuff back—that was where my head was at. And I definitely got the vibe that he had an issue with women, particularly women with strong personalities.

There was only one other woman who would report to him in OS. She and I had crossed paths in the past.

His first official action as the Deputy was to spend money, that we had not budgeted for, on redoing an office so he could have a precious window.

People notice these things. They notice when a leader does things that are not aligned with our values. I guess at that level, he felt entitled to a window.

We butted heads on just about everything.

He fixated on the fact that I was a first-year senior executive. Never mind the 25 years of organizational experience I had to get there, the multiple times I acted in SES positions for extensive periods, and the fact that you have to display the core qualifications and have done work to meet them before becoming an SES.

He didn't listen to learn; he listened to respond and criticize. He quickly developed a reputation among the women as a condescending prick. It wasn't just me. If it were, I would think I needed to fix something. But it was not. He was definitely the problem.

Before he came on board, the previous regime had me fill in for them on Department level meetings quite often. This continued whenever he was not around. It was common for me to call in and just listen. His boss would ask me to cover if he wasn't going to be there.

I also had the role of providing a CBP operational update as the XD of my Directorate on a recurring basis. This was still a pandemic timeframe, so these meetings were held virtually.

On one particular meeting, during which the Deputy was supposed to be on leave, I was asked to cover. To my surprise, he was on the meeting. He saw that I was also on and confronted me after as to why. I explained that I was asked to cover for him and didn't know he would be on and that I usually provided the briefing.

To which he responded, "I'm the Deputy, this is a Deputy level meeting and that is my role."

Yikes, ok. I always felt dejected and dismissed after speaking with him. I had to learn my place. I thought, I'm a team player; your boss asked me to sit in on the meeting. He constantly confronted me. He didn't like how I briefed, we disagreed on the outcomes required of certain projects, and it chaffed him to no end that his boss consistently depended on me to get things done.

We continued our tet-a-tet.

He would often slip up in emails and say something condescending or even mean, while others were copied on it, including his boss and the Chief of Staff — which was an amazing day for me. Finally, they saw what I was dealing with. After one such back and forth, he asked his assistant to find time on my calendar for a one-on-one in-person meeting. He was probably told to do so. I still went into the office every day, so that would not be an issue for me.

I walked into his office, adorned with treasures he had acquired over the years on his diplomatic assignments and sat by the door — a good 20 feet from him. This is how he had it set up — there were no chairs any closer to his desk, not that I still wouldn't have chosen one that was furthest away. We were still in a pandemic, and I felt the need to be as far away from his person as I could manage.

He opened up with what almost sounded like an apology, but instead, what he said was worse than the first thing he'd ever said to me.

He asserted that he expected me to get in line, not push back, not provide alternate realities, options or my opinion. What he said goes. Period. He was the boss. I needed to fall in line and essentially be a "yes man."

I listened, seething inside. I would not, have never been and never will be a "Yes man." I'm not even a man!

I told him I had no confusion about the chain of command, but I didn't agree with him on many things and we would have to find a way to deal with that. He simply was not always right, regardless of his rank.

I told him that I would no longer sit in a room alone with him and I wanted a witness to every conversation we had whether in person or via email. He said different things when we were alone than what he portrayed to others.

His entire facial expression dropped to the floor and the color drained from his face. I think I scared him. I did, for a short time, consider filing an EEO—I most assuredly felt he was treating me differently than any of the men. I knew he was. He did the same to the other women. I was inches from filing that day. I already had a POC and spoken to them to see if I had any legitimate reason to file.

The straw that broke the camel's back was around performance rating time. As an executive, you have 5 core competencies that you are rated against. There are performance goals within each of those competencies and you work your derriere off trying to get the highest rating you can.

Nothing less than exceptional is acceptable, to me anyway. Each executive prepares their assessment of their actions and outcomes to meet their goals and provides a 5-page document to their supervisor to be rated.

It is pretty difficult to fit a year's worth of accomplishments into 5 pages, with enough detail to make sense. This document takes weeks to prepare. He gave me a less-than-stellar rating in two of the competencies.

I don't even think he read my assessment. I think he went through and rated me based on our interactions.

I had never received a performance rating that wasn't damn good and I prided myself on my work ethic. I was dependable and given a lot of projects and opportunities over my career that were not easy tasks. I worked so flipping hard to accomplish every goal in my plan.

I was pissed.

I asked for a meeting with him to discuss my rating because I did not agree with it. I prepared my butt off for that meeting. I presented my accomplishments line by line.

One of his comments was that one of my major accomplishments was completed before he arrived and the prior Deputy, on her way out, told him he didn't need to worry about it. I thought, 'Exactly — if it's assigned to me, you do not need to worry about it.' I think that was her way of hoping he wouldn't stick his nose in and jack it up.

WHAT? So that doesn't count? Pardon me for being efficient. He changed the rating in that competency. I said, ok, what about this other one?

In his overarching comments at the end of the plan he mentioned something about being a first-year executive which only pissed me off more. It ground on my nerves that he was so fixated on that. I asked why it mattered. He did not have a good reason. He essentially said that no first-year SES should get the highest rating.

What kind of asinine reasoning is that? Again, I had to prove myself worthy of the senior executive level in government to get the position and now tenure is a factor is my performance? I could not understand it. Never mind that I was into my second year as an executive, but first full rating year according to him.

He said, "You mean to tell me you've learned everything you need to as an executive."

Nowhere in my plan nor any of my statements did I say or insinuate that. I set goals; I accomplished those goals, some of them above and beyond. What does that have to do with learning new things. Of course, I have more to learn. We all do!

However, serendipity struck.

That same day, the Chief of the Border Patrol called me to come and see him when I had a chance. He wanted to discuss something.

I had a great team and we were making progress. I was happy with my work. I was content. I wasn't stressed — except by this a-hole of a boss. The Chief struck while that iron was hot.

He asked if I wanted to come back to the Border Patrol.

I said maybe, but not in uniform.

He agreed that I had already "been there, done that" as far as operations were concerned. He offered me two choices, so I took the one where I saw an opportunity to finally make some changes that would positively benefit the agents and professional staff employees — the Mission Support Directorate. It was hard to leave my team; we had created a great environment, made a lot of progress, and had incredible comradery. I did cry that day.

I was admittedly a bit mentally broken when I took this position. 24 years of operational crisis had taken its toll. I was working on myself and healing.

I went from "I don't want to do this anymore," to "I'm not doing this anymore."

In retrospect, I could have shown more grace toward my old Deputy. I could have tried harder to get along with him. I had to prove myself in every position I took throughout my career — and it was exhausting. When I came into this position, I didn't feel as if I would have to prove myself as much — my boss, the woman who hired me already had full confidence in my abilities. Yet, here I was.

I didn't have the patience for toxic leadership anymore. I could not work in an environment where I was not allowed any autonomy.

I think he was paranoid too — after learning a little about his upbringing. He was bullied too and I started to feel some empathy. It certainly explained a lot about him.

Nevertheless, I'm not one to pull any punches. Don't ask me a question if you don't want a straight answer.

After requesting that he not attend my going away, and not contact me; he still attended my going away and he still sent me a goodbye email and opened the door with, "I hope I'm not in any part a reason why you're leaving."

I straight up told him he was the one and only reason I was leaving.

He tried to apologize. He had a daughter, so, he couldn't possibly have a problem with women—that means nothing, buddy. I was told a few years later that he confided in a mutual acquaintance that he felt he handled the situation badly. He did.

Hollow and too little too late.

Gaining a new perspective and appreciation for Professional Staff.

Although my departure wasn't prefaced on a great recent experience, it was a nice 18-month vacation from the chaos of the Border Patrol. Overall, the experience was good and it helped to broaden my exposure, knowledge and network throughout DHS.

Back to the Border Patrol I went.

I was going home, to a place I knew well, and I knew I was respected and understood. Once again, however, entering into a position I felt wholly unprepared for. I would be the first Executive Director in this position who had also been a Border Patrol Agent. I wasn't a lifetime professional staffer, mission support expert, or any of the like. I knew the basic surface information about the administrative side of the house from my prior law enforcement positions. But I had no idea the scope, complexity, dedication, and hard work that the professional staff put into this organization.

Agents and Chiefs of Sectors, many of who were my peer group coming up through the agency, were excited to see a former LEO in the role. Although I never heard this, I can only imagine what the lifetime professional staffers must have thought. 'GREAT—an operator coming in here who is going to try and change everything and tell us how things should be done.'

I would not be that person though.

Within the Mission Support Directorate (MSD), there were 7 divisions: Budget/Finance, Property and Procurement (which included the national fleet program), Recruiting, Resiliency, Training, Workforce Management (I.E. Human Resources), and last but not least Facilities. Essentially everything that makes up the foundation of the organization so that operators can operate.

I mean, if I'm being honest, they could not do what they do without mission support. Money, tactical supplies (guns, radios, handcuffs, tasers), vehicles and buildings—some things a lot of people failed to realize.

I truly believe, in order to become the Chief of a Sector, people should have to do at a minimum 6 months in national level Mission Support. It would really open their eyes to the realities of this scope of work and make them better leaders.

Professional staff are often looked down upon by uniformed agents. I don't know why, but there is this attitude among a lot of agents that if you're not a gun-toter, you are less than.

I felt this—if I went into a room or a meeting and folks didn't know my name, they would automatically gloss over me, and not really give me a second look. Especially, if there was a uniformed agent in our presence.

Until I was introduced (as the person who controls the budget—*evil laugh*), they recognized my name, OR someone mentioned that I was once an agent, I was second fiddle. Maybe even third, or not acknowledged at all. Ouch. There is an automatic credibility given to someone in uniform.

Leaving Leaders in Place—Making it Awkward.

This would be another scenario where I was coming into a team whose current leader—acting in the role I was about to take over—had been in the highest leadership position of the directorate for over a year, was staying on and going back to their day job, so to speak.

She was technically the Deputy, but when the former XD left, she took over his duties. She drove it like she owned it, as she should have. She had also applied for, interviewed for, and was tentatively selected for the position. She was well liked, wicked smart, well respected and had made a lot of progress in bringing the other directorates (including operations) together to behave as a team, which is an incredibly challenging task.

It was a true peer partnership between the four national directorates that made up Border Patrol HQ and that was largely due to her efforts. For reasons that are not mine or anyone else's business, her offer for the position was rescinded and I came in a short time later. She would stay on as my Deputy.

Awkward. How did I keep getting put in this position?

She and I had worked together on the periphery before I left the Border Patrol 18 months earlier, while I was acting in the national Deputy for operations position. We were peers then. From what I heard coming back in, she was glad it was me, someone she already knew, taking over the directorate, if it couldn't be her.

I went into the position respecting the fact that she had already done the job I was about to do. She was a lifetime professional staffer and truly, if I'm being completely honest, more qualified for this job than I was. But don't count me out, I'm a quick learner.

What I brought to the table was an established relationship with. and intimate knowledge of, field operations. I could call BS on Sector Chiefs and their claims, but I also knew how to provide interpretation of operational speak to professional staff and administrative processes to operators. I could grease the skids, be an intermediary, explain the why, and so on.

I wanted us to be a dynamic duo — true partners in the running of the directorate. I was hesitant to step on her toes. I would come to realize that approach was a mistake. With no clear roles and responsibilities between our positions, it really just confused everyone and strained our working relationship.

While we had generally the same idea of where we wanted to see the Directorate go, strategy wise, we had very different leadership and implementation styles. I felt that she still had her agenda from the time she spent in the XD role, which come to find out didn't totally align with mine.

It came to blows one day while we were discussing something she had done that she shouldn't have, which reached the highest levels of the organization and pissed people off.

She said to me, "Maybe I should just leave and find something else." I agreed, which shocked her.

I'm not going to beg someone to stay who doesn't want to be there, and frankly, I needed a deputy — not someone I felt was constantly fighting me for control. She did end up leaving, which I hope has worked out to be a much better scenario for her and her family.

I had clear expectations for my time left in the Border Patrol. It was already 2023, a very quick 12 months from eligibility. I wanted to fix some of the lesser supportive elements of employee care and resiliency, and structure the budget so that Sectors felt like they were being supported with transparency into the process. The prior permanent XD did some funky things with the budget—constantly robbing Peter to pay Paul—which turned out was something we couldn't avoid. But he would also "tax" the Sectors to pay for HQ programs or initiatives. I had been on the receiving end of those arbitrary budget cuts, leaving sectors with barely enough funds to function and I was intent on putting an end to it.

If I learned anything of value in my time as the XD over Mission Support, it's the incredible work that our professional staff does for the agency.

I don't have the adequate vocabulary to truly put into words the deep appreciation and affection for them as humans. Also, for the pressure they face, the abuse they take, and the fact that they carry on and continue to succeed, regardless. A truly incredible scope of responsibilities that is not seen.

It's almost all behind the scenes and they frankly get nowhere near the recognition and appreciation that they deserve. My hats off to professional staff.

Chapter 18
Beards, Tattoos and Pony Tails

Honest to God, one of the longest and most emotionally charged arguments throughout my time in the Border Patrol was over whether or not agents should be allowed to have beards and tattoos.

There are two camps of thought—beards and tattoos are unprofessional, reserved for gangsters and low lifers. Or beards and tattoos are fine, period, no issue. What I find hilariously ironic is that nearly every male agent after they retire wears a full beard as soon as they can grow it in.

The era of the hipster really changed a large portion of society's viewpoint on beards and tattoos, along with just the general social acceptance over time.

I have tattoos. All of my kids have tattoos and we're all decent human beings. Tattooing is a huge industry and you can barely find someone over the age of 18 without one these days. Beards are a trend that will come and go for most.

The camp that finds beards unprofessional have a visceral reaction to the conversation every single time. The topic of beards became a bargaining chip between management and the union during the last renegotiation of the bargaining unit contract. I mean, the union seriously could have fought for so many worthwhile things that could have actually benefitted all employees, but they chose this fight—for the men who wanted to grow a beard.

I personally don't mind a well-kept beard. After seeing all the things I've seen in my career, I'm much more concerned about the character of a person. Whether or not a man has a beard tells me absolutely nothing about their character.

Once the contract was settled on, it only applied to bargaining unit employees — not management.

So, the argument turned to whether or not to allow supervisors and above to grow beards. Holy Moly, it was a fight at every single Chief's conference for at least the 2 years I was in the XD position.

Since we were already arguing about beards, I decided to throw the tattoo conversation into the fire. Hehe! Yeah, let's burn this mother to the ground.

My Chief at the time got very tired of talking about tattoos, the same Chief that came along with me on the support K-9 idea. I pushed his boundaries sometimes. Often times.

He would look at me and say, "Kathleen, we're not talking about tattoos today." Yes, sir.

He didn't want to be the one to make that decision. He was about to retire and I think he just couldn't get there, in his mind.

The collective leadership in the organization could not agree either, but I soon saw an opportunity to get decisions made.

We had a new Chief, who I had known and worked with over the years, and I already had a certain comfort level with him. We had a one-on-one meeting, once a month and after one such meeting where I presented a number of items that were on my plate requiring decisions, he said to email him. I emailed him that afternoon.

To my extreme surprise, he responded that same evening with a decision on every single item I presented. Halle-fricken-luja! I wasn't about to ask any questions.

If I'd learned one thing over time, when a Chief decides, you run with it, before they change their mind.

At the next Chief's conference, while I was presenting the decisions to the Sector Chiefs — shit got really uncomfortable.

Not only would beards be allowed for managers, we were radically changing our tattoo allowance policies. Previously, agents could have tattoos, but not on their necks, hands, or faces. And they had to be covered when wearing dress uniform if they had tattoo sleeves, for example. Obviously, nothing offensive or gang related was allowed to be visible. Not that agents should have gang tattoos anyway — you've got a much bigger problem if that's the case. Additionally, I was announcing several employee support transfer initiatives that we were putting in place.

The tattoo policies over time went from no policy to grandfathering in tattoos that agents already had when polices went into effect — without an accountability mechanism and no true way to prove they had it prior or not. Agents had started getting tattooed all over their bodies — newer generations and younger agents — so we needed to get our shit sorted.

We had trainees showing up to the academy, being forced to agree to remove tattoos, thus scarring their bodies, just to be a Border Patrol Agent. They had to have the tattoo removed prior to attending, in some cases.

Let me say that again — *we were asking people to permanently scar their bodies so they could be a Border Patrol Agent.*

I don't know if a tattoo of your dearly departed brother's name on your neck actually looks worse than a scar.

Tattoo removal is neither cheap, fast, nor painless. And some sectors were granting waivers, which made any application of the policy super inconsistent when waivers were never allowed for anyway.

Might as well cut this albatross off before we end up with a lawsuit. We were enforcing the policy on some people and not others. We were making future agents remove a cross tattoo from their hand and allowing someone already in the agency to go in public, on video, with a neck tattoo, front and center – even though the policy didn't allow neck tattoos. Completely contradictory. Didn't seem right in my mind.

The military had already changed their policies – some allowing neck and hand tattoos. The USBP has a large contingent of veterans that come into the agency, with over 20% of all agents being veterans.

So, were we going to exclude people who decided to get a tattoo (their kid's name for example), who have served our country – from becoming a Border Patrol Agent? We were having a hard enough time finding recruits as it was!

I was also in charge of recruiting and we were not meeting the numbers needed to keep up with attrition. My stance was that we really needed to move into the 21st century and catch up with societal changes if we were going to be a competitive law enforcement agency. Other state and local law enforcement agencies were changing their policies. Tattoos and beards are no longer reserved for those on the fringes of society.

At this Chief's conference, one Chief in particular, Tom, an old patroller (super angry, loved to argue) decided to open his mouth.

I always knew I could depend on Tom to provide feedback (i.e. argue) against any change. There were typically 20-30 people in attendance at these quarterly meetings – 20 sector Chiefs, as well as the HQ Directorate Chiefs and XDs and the national level Chief and Deputy, of course. About half never said a word.

Tom went off about one thing or another at every single conference. A few others would jump on the bandwagon or get him fired up.

I could see his face turning bright red as he sat there shaking his head. He'd already had one heart attack; I was hoping he wasn't going to have another right then and there about beards and tattoos.

Incidentally, he was one of my journeymen in Nogales when I was a trainee. He was a good agent and a good journeyman, for the most part – I learned a lot with him.

He thought he was funny, however, at my expense. We were out tracking a group and returned to our truck after a long hike during the day shift in the hot Arizona summer. I was taking a drink from my blue Gatorade as we made our way out of the canyon we were in. We were moving along when he hit the brakes hard, for no apparent reason, just as I lifted the bottle to my mouth to take a drink, thus spilling blue Gatorade down the front of my uniform and all up in my face. Up my nose, down my shirt. Ah, that's the reason he hit the brakes. Dick! I was glad it was close to the end of shift. I really didn't want to be out in the heat with sticky Gatorade attracting every insect in the desert.

Tom had turned into an angry curmudgeon stuck in the old patrol mindset. Come to think of it, he was always kind of grumpy.

He asked, "Why should we lower our standards? If people want to be Border Patrol Agents, they can meet our standards."

That was the general argument against any change.

I said, "I'm not sure what *standards* you're trying to maintain by not allowing beards or tattoos. We have a lot bigger problems to worry about, like agents committing suicide."

We didn't require people to BYOH (bring your own horse) anymore – one of the requirements of the first agents back in the 1920s – and now we were prejudging someone based on a beard or tattoo?

I turned away from the table of Chiefs, removing my sweater to reveal the tattoos along my shoulders and upper back.

"What exactly are you inferring about people with tattoos?" I asked.

I could hide them if I wanted to or not. I didn't get my first tattoo until I was in my 30s – and when people meet me, for whatever reason, they are surprised to learn I have tattoos.

No comments from the peanut gallery. I do love a dramatic mic drop.

Tom argued that we had lost our bargaining chips, as he wanted to be able to use certain program ideas (the transfer programs, in particular) as those bargaining chips during the next round of negotiations with the union – whenever that was going to be – years down the line. He also *hated* beards on agents, but he'd worn a mustache for as long as I could remember.

He was part of the last party of managers that agreed to beards during union negotiations but "By God, Supervisors shouldn't be allowed to have them."

He thought that he was going to put me on the spot with that. I asked why we should wait to do what was right for our agents. If we can do it, we should do it. Why wait for years; years where agents would continue to leave the agency because they weren't supported, when we have the power to fix it right now? And, also, the union wouldn't get credit for 'making' management do the right thing, if we already did it. There was already a large contingent of agents that routinely complained about a lack of support from managers.

Sputter, sputter – he couldn't argue with that.

Then he asked whether or not the tattoo decision was final.

I turned to the Chief – who'd made the decision.

I looked at him and said, "Chief?"

All I could think in my head at the time was you better not fricken waiver. Wanna step up here buddy? I'm in the line of fire without backup at the moment.

To his credit, the Chief stood his ground and stated the obvious, "We can talk about this for years to come and never come to consensus." I personally appreciated, and stated so, that someone had decided one way or the other.

I didn't really care what the decision was, but that it was made and we could move forward and stop talking about it. Next contestant?

Can I just tell you, that the month after managers were allowed to grow beards, no less than half of the Sector Chiefs and Deputies were sporting them – along with a large percentage of all of management.

They still have to shave them off if they are going to be in dress uniform. Compromise.

Last, but not least, on this particular list of emotionally charged topics: ponytails.

Where and how were women being represented in this fight? They really weren't, if we're being honest. Well, women have tattoos too, but I have yet to find one that can or wants to grow a beard.

What the women did want was to be able to wear their hair in a ponytail. As opposed to the current regulations that required the hair to be off the collar, somehow constrained to their head – in a bun, or some other contraption that didn't allow it to be free flowing in any way.

Women with heavy, thick, coarse, or natural hair often complained of headaches and hair loss from having to wear their hair in tight buns all the time. The one and only argument I ever heard against ponytails since my academy days, almost always from a man, was this: "It's a safety concern."

Someone can grab you by your ponytail and if they control your head, they control you. Pretty sure someone could grab my bun, too.

I bought it for a long time. Makes some sense, actually. But then I started thinking – who says? Where does this come from? Is there any empirical evidence that shows this to be the case? Are there any cases, during which a female officer or agent, in any department, was a victim of such?

No? No data, nothing? Interesting.

If you can't wear a ponytail and don't have to wear a bun, I don't want to hear from you for the rest of the day.

Ok, we allowed the men beards. Let's give the women ponytails.

And we did.

I can hear the retired old patrollers now. "What has happened to my beloved patrol?"

Even some of the women who were self-proclaimed traditionalists started wearing ponytails. "This is actually kind of nice," they'd say.

Moving a very-slow-to-change organization forward is exhausting. I hated briefing at these conferences because everything under my purview was emotional for the Sector Chiefs – money, people, and assets.

Everyone wanted, and needed, more. And there was only so much to go around.

So. Many. Feelings. *Shiver.*

Chapter 19
Let's Wrap It Up and Start A New Chapter

I'm sure you can tell the change in the tone of my writing as I've gotten into some of these later topics. It's not as easy to write – I was growing weary; tired of arguing, tired of trying to educate people who just weren't open to listen, learn or change their minds or their ways.

My job had turned into a chore that wasn't enjoyable anymore. I felt a responsibility to the people of the organization, to my team, and the incredible work they were doing; but I had sacrificed a lot in the last 27 years.

Very grown-up feelings. Blech! I used the other F word.

Shortly after my 49th birthday, I made a decision. I would retire the month I turned 50.

Honestly, once the support K-9 program was established, I felt like, 'That's it I don't need to accomplish anything else in my career. That was the absolute pinnacle.'

I don't know if people thought I was going to stick around forever. I was somewhat of a staple in the organization – both my husband and I were. People were shocked when I shifted into the civilian position – but also encouraged me.

A number of folks asked me about it and realized it may be a good move for them as well. People were double shocked when I finally announced – a month before my final date – that I was actually retiring. I kept it as quiet as I could because I just didn't want to deal with all the questions. Rumors were percolating anyway.

People would say, "I heard you're retiring."

I would just answer, "Well, I'm eligible in February."

I still had work to do and did not want people around me, to think that they could wait me out if they knew I was leaving. I also didn't want anyone to change my mind as I was searching for a job outside government. I didn't want to be hassled by companies offering big money for something I didn't necessarily want to do or with a company that wasn't great to work for.

Senior Executives coming out of government are a bit of a commodity to industry, particularly in the Washington, DC area where most of private industry is focused on government contracting work. I had contacts with recently retired agents who were, number one, trustworthy and would keep it on the down low. And number two, willing to make connections for folks getting ready to retire.

One of my connections secured a meeting with an individual, Patty, who knows both the industry landscape and Government. She is a wealth of true and good information. Patty helped me to find potential companies, was honest about how they treated their people, and helped me sort out where my best fit would be. She hooked me up with a company that was looking to expand their government contract portfolio and I had the right subject matter expertise they were looking for.

The hiring process was a very different scenario than anything I had ever experienced in the government. The interviews were really just discussions, and I believe my reputation was speaking for me, as well as a few references the company relied on.

I should note that this is an Information Technology (IT) company and I know very little about IT. I know how to log onto my computer and I know how to turn it off and back on again if something isn't functioning properly – but that is about it. Technology intimidates me.

My first interview felt like the man I was meeting with (who would become my future boss) was selling the company to me instead of me sharing what I may have to offer.

The meeting was held over brunch in the booth of a restaurant.

I then had a meeting/interview with their human resources executive and again, she really put me at ease. So different than that original Border Patrol interview.

I was offered an opportunity to speak at an event in the fall before I retired that the company was sponsoring. I believe this was Patty's way of showing the company that I could hold my own and make relative associations between my work and their industry. She had become a great champion of mine throughout this process.

I talked about recruiting – not an IT thing at all – but even the OIT folks in the room from CBP high-fived me after. I really have no recollection of what I said that deserved high-fives.

I can turn it on when I need to. I'm much more comfortable in front of a microphone now than I ever was earlier in my career.

Several months later, I accepted a position as a Vice President of Operations in one of their business units and started work 2 days after I officially retired from Government. My foundational circumstances won't yet allow me to go without the security of a paycheck.

The tech industry is intimidating; these people are incredibly intelligent. I know I have the ability to learn quickly, but please don't ask me anything related to IT. I'm learning a whole new language in acronyms alone.

Here I go again – feeling wholly unprepared for what lies ahead of me – but hey, it's worked out so far. I'll figure it out. I'm always up for a challenge.

I didn't cry at my retirement.

I was all smiles, a bit of a departure from how most people saw me on a daily basis. In fact, it may have been the truest happiness I had felt in a very long time. Chappie, the poodle was there – maybe that helped too. I'd seen the macho-ist of men cry at their retirements, but I was not even remotely emotional in that sense. Which just helped to solidify in my mind that it was time.

I had a line on my email signature for a long time that read: *Leadership isn't about position; it is about behavior.* I don't know who said it originally or I would give credit to that person, but it spoke to me. People often asked what my leadership philosophy was – that was it. Pretty simple.

I believe that is also my life philosophy. It doesn't matter who you are at work, what position you hold, because one day that ends. People won't remember a damn thing you said to them, but they will always remember how you treated them and how that made them feel. You never know what someone is dealing with and you might just need them someday.

So, yeah, don't be a dick.